DEDICATION

Dedicated to Herb Lepp

· ·

CONTENTS

• •

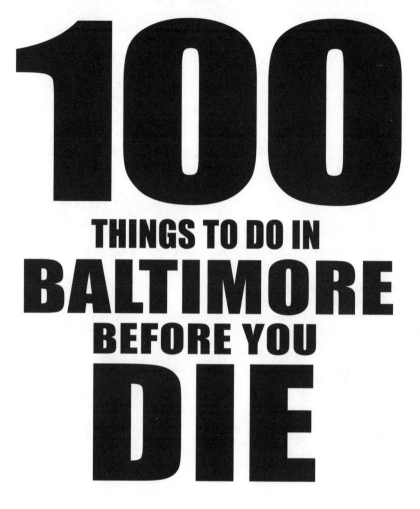

100

THINGS TO DO IN
BALTIMORE
BEFORE YOU
DIE

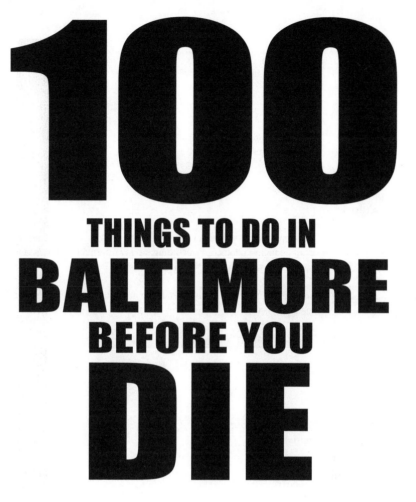

100

THINGS TO DO IN
BALTIMORE
BEFORE YOU
DIE

JUDY COLBERT

REEDY PRESS

Library of Congress Control Number: 2015942717

ISBN: 9781681060132

Design by Jill Halpin

Cover and interior photos: Judy Colbert
Author headshot: Stan Ruddie

Printed in the United States of America
16 17 18 19 20   5 4 3 2 1

Please note that websites, phone numbers, addresses, and company names are subject to change or cancellation. We did our best to relay the most accurate information available, but due to circumstances beyond our control, please do not hold us liable for misinformation. When exploring new destinations, please do your homework before you go.

Music and Entertainment

● ●

Sports and Recreation

Culture and History

• •

• •

Shopping and Fashion

PREFACE

Whether you're a local (approximately 620,000 within the city limits) or a visitor (about 24 million annually), there's too much to see and do in Baltimore in any one lifetime. There's world-class art to see and experience, world-class food to enjoy, and walking, biking, boating, shopping, and listening (to nature and amateur/professional musicians) to do. The events that take place here can fill their own book, from the first Light City to fireworks to the lights along the Miracle on 34th Street. One great thing about Baltimore is it's a year-round city and there are things to see and do regardless of the weather (okay, stay indoors during the occasional hurricane or blizzard).

This book, one in a series of *100 Things to Do* books about cities across the United States, tries to help you decide what to see and do by dividing the city into five categories: Food and Drink, Music and Entertainment, Sports and Recreation, Culture and History, and Shopping and Fashion. And, although the book's title says 100 Things, there are more because I cheated and listed a few places where you can do the same thing (as in where to try pit beef or crab cakes or watch fireworks at the Inner Harbor). So many of Baltimore's attractions are unique to Charm City and there's so much of which we should be proud. Almost all of them are within the city limits; however a few go beyond that. Well worth the drive, if they do.

Baltimore is known for several foods, particularly Bergers cookies, chocolates, coddies, Chesapeake Bay blue crabs (as in steamed crabs, soft or softshell crabs, Maryland crab soup, Maryland she-crab soup, crab pretzels, crab pizza, crab Benedict or crab cake Benedict, crab fries, crab dip, Old Bay ice cream sandwiches—with crab cakes as the sandwich part—and the list continues), corned beef, sauerkraut, bull and oyster roasts, Tulkoff's horseradish, Lady Baltimore cake, pit beef, and snowballs (or snoballs or sno-balls, but NOT snowcones, Italian ices, or Hawaiian shave ice). The lemon peppermint stick is also a favorite, usually found at school PTA fairs and similar fun and fundraising events. To make one, simply roll a lemon across a kitchen counter or table to help get it juicy, cut it in half, and insert a straight piece of peppermint stick (not a candy cane) and suck (pucker) away. Enjoy!

If you want to start a lively discussion, simply state—in your most affirmative voice—which restaurant or food joint has the best crab cake, softshells, etc. You know, without question, that you make the best, but that's another story. I wrote a cookbook about Chesapeake Bay crabs that has 123 recipes in it, including eighteen recipes for crab cakes and several for crab soup. As I know there's only one BEST recipe for each, the others are frivolous, but it would have been a much thinner cookbook without them. You can even find an argument in whether Old Bay spices or some other brand is best.

I know I've not included everything. My original idea list totaled more than 150 items, and that was just the beginning. Please let me know what you enjoy and what should be included in the next edition.

Love!

Judy Colbert

•   •

ACKNOWLEDGMENTS

A great deal of thanks goes to dozens of people who helped with suggestions and inside tips. I hope I haven't forgotten anyone. My appreciation goes to: Adam Paul, Adette McCormick, Aleia Hendricks, Amanda Davis, Angela Carter, Barbara Green Kreft, Barbara J. Mitchell, Betty Phillips, Bill Corbin, Bill Moniodis, Bob Young, Bob Willis, Brian Manieri, Brian Sindler, Brent Manns, Carmen Limongello Cook, Carmen Strollo, Carol Sorgen, Charlie Merkey, Charlotte Hays Murray, Connie Spindler Yingling, Craig Healy, Darlene Sunshine, Dave Croft, Dave Rollhauser, Daven Bridgewater, David Smith, Deanna Martino, Dee Herget, Denise Bowling Miller, Dian Hullett, Dianne Trinite Rudolph, Don Lombardi, Donna Marine, Elaine Eff, Ernest Miller, Fran Koch, Francine Pierce, Frank Krach, Glenn D. Glenn, Glyndia Clark, Heather Fisher Noll, Helen Snider, Holly Crouse, Jacqueline Neun, James Bush, Janet Pettaway, Jennifer Marie Moran, Jim Dixon, Jimmy Tochterman, John and Mari Karabelas, John Jung, Jon Randall, Judie Greenwood, Justus Heger, Karen Cosgrove Enoch, Karri Snyder, Karrie Lynn Hylock Hogan, Kass Sichette, Kathryn Waters, Kev Jenk, Kim Nagle Quinn, Kimberly Diane, Kitty Stallings-Harrison, Latisha Jones, Lesa Bauersfeld-Cason, Lisa Blatcher, Loretta Ruckle, Lorraine Standiford Branick, Mark Whiteford, Mary Hanna Clofelter, Mary Tranelllo, Mary Trimper

• •

DeCastro, Matt Biagioli, Matt Potochnik, Melissa Heaver, Melodie Banknell Deacon, Michael R K Cavey, Michael Shay, Michelle Mikki Evans, Mike Carista, Mike Kap, Monee Cottman, Monica Good, Monika Gibbons, Nancy Himes, Nina Hatlem-Ward, Nina Nicole Williams, Pam Lauer, Pam Williams, Paula Hankins, Phil Johnston, Rashida Martin, Regina Angeles, Rhoda Burrell, Richard Lange, Rick Plantholt, Robert Clemons, Roger Hartley, Ronald Simmont, Roswell Encina, Scott Gunther, Sharon Doerr Dingus, Sharon Maddox, Shawn White, Stacy Seidman Greenstreet, Steve Winger, Sue H. Hunter, Sue Papke, Susan Elgert Keffer, Susan Lloyd, Susan Trombetti, Sylvia Young, Tina Ferguson, Tom Wagers, Victoria Figueroa, Wesley Wilson, and William W. Sharp.

• •

FOOD AND DRINK

CHOCK FULL OF NUTS
AND CREAMS AND CHERRIES AND ...

Louis and Esther Rheb started making their eponymous chocolates in their home in 1917. Win and Patricia Harger are the third generation to provide these delectable goodies. With as many as forty people preparing the sweets during the holidays, the chocolates are always fresh and waiting to melt in your mouth. The dark chocolate vanilla buttercreams and the Jimmy truffles are fan favorites, but you should let your taste buds explore other flavors so you can make your final decision. Yes, they have candies other than chocolates. Rheb's Chocolates are sold only at their Wilkens Avenue store and online.

Rheb's Homemade Chocolates, 3352 Wilkens Ave.
410-644-4321, rhebcandy.com/321

MEMORIES THAT WILL WARM THE COCKLES OF
YOUR HEART (OR TUMMY)

The only argument you'll hear about coddies is whether people love or hate them. According to Gilbert Sandler in his *Glimpses of Jewish Baltimore,* they started in the Jewish community, more than one hundred years ago. Louis and Fannie Jacobson Cohen started Cohen's Coddies in 1910, selling them through the early 1970s. "Trucks were delivering coddies all over town," says Sandler. A mixture of codfish and mashed potatoes, they're breaded, fried, and served with yellow mustard between two Saltine crackers. Geresbeck's groceries sell them as do some churches on Fridays during Lent. Other locations with coddies on the menu are:

Attman's Delicatessen ($1.69 each), 1019 E Lombard St.
(also in Cabin John, Montgomery County)
410-563-2666, attmansdeli.com

Mama's on the Half Shell (three coddies for $8), 2901 O'Donnell St.
410-276-3160, mamasmd.com/MamasSite/

Pappas Restaurant & Sports Bar (four coddies for $12)
1725 Taylor Ave. Parkville, (also in Cockeysville and Glen Burnie)
410-661-4357, pappascrabcakes.com/restaurants

EVERYTHING'S
COMING UP BACON

If you follow food and drink trends, you've probably heard of one of Baltimore's best-known dive bars, Bad Decisions. It's a Fells Point bar whose Beer & Bacon Nights have made them famous. Generally, they have one every month—check their Facebook page for updates—when everything bacon is featured. Order a LARGE snifter of crispy bacon. Maybe there's a bacon-habanero mojito or a bacon-crab bloody Mary. You can try bacon mac and cheese, bacon deviled eggs, or a roasted corn and bacon bisque. One never knows where or how bacon will appear on the food or drink menu. They have the requisite beers, craft cocktails, and food served in plastic baskets. Owner John Reusing started Bad Decisions after a time as a bartender when the bar's owner didn't like any of his ideas. Seems he had a good idea with this popular place.

Bad Decisions, 701 S Bond St.
410-979-5161, makeabaddecision.com

TIP

They also have Sunday and Monday brunch
with a changing menu, and a variety of rare top-shelf
selections including aged Scotch and other rarities.
Service can be uneven at times, but it seems to excel on
the Bacon & Beer Nights.

WHEN THERE'S NO
TIME TO PICK

G & M Restaurant in Linthicum Heights (just outside the Beltway) continues to rank high and highest in any crab cake competition. They're popular enough that G & M ships them near and far. Weighing in at eight ounces, I like to say they're held together with imagination rather than filler. They're baked, not fried. During weekday lunch and weekend dinner, expect to wait. Don't worry, it's worth it. Desserts look scrumptious. I wouldn't know because I'm already stuffed. The place is packed at lunch, generally with badge-wearing employees from the nearby No Such Agency (National Security Agency).

G & M Restaurant, 804 N Hammonds Ferry Rd.
877-554-3723, gandmcrabcakes.com

Faidley Seafood Lexington Market 203 North Paca St.
410-727-4898, faidleyscrabcakes.com

Koco's Pub, 4301 Harford Rd.
410-426-3519, kocospub.com

Thames Street Oyster House, 1728 Thames St., Fells Point
443-449-7726, thamesstreetoysterhouse.com

Here are a few choices for hard crabs:

Canton Dockside
3301 Boston St., Canton
410-276-8900, cantondockside.com

Captain James Landing
2127 Boston St., Canton
410-675-1819 (crab house & carry out)
410-327-8600 (restaurant)
captainjameslanding.com

CJ'S Crabhouse and Grill
10117 Reisterstown Rd., Owings Mills
410-363-6694, cjscrabs.com

Costas Inn
4100 Northpoint Blvd.
410-477-1975, costasinn.com

L.P. Steamers
1100 E. Fort Ave.
410-576-9294, locustpointsteamers.com

JUST PICKIN' THE
NIGHT AWAY

Unless you can't or don't eat crustaceans, you must try hard shell crabs. It's a several-hour social event. It's done on brown craft paper, with a hammer and nutcracker, a pitcher or more of beer, some buttered corn on the cob, and lots of friends. Eat in or take them home. Buy them already steamed or steam them yourself. So many options. How to decide where to go? What's closest to you? Whose spices are best (not everyone uses Old Bay)? What other food is available for non-crab eaters? How much do the crabs cost? Have fun!

TIP

Chesapeake Bay crabs are seasonal.
You can buy crabs year-round, but in
the winter, they'll be from the Carolinas or the
Gulf of Mexico. Basically, the same crab,
but they've done some traveling.

IT'S DEFINITELY
THE PITS

Pit beef is a cross between BBQ and roast beef that's been grilled over a charcoal fire, sliced thin, and piled mouth-high, usually on a Kaiser roll. It's definitely charred rare. An almost unanimous vote in an unscientific Facebook poll names Chaps Famous Pit Beef the hands-down favorite. Gus and Bob started the place in 1987 with beef, ham, and sausage but no electricity or phone. The original twelve-by-fifteen-foot shack has grown and the menu expanded (you can even buy t-shirts and other apparel). Thanks to coverage on several national television shows, their reputation extends way beyond city and county lines.

Chaps Charcoal Restaurant 5801 Pulaski Hwy.
410-483-2379, chapspitbeef.com/index.php

Also in Aberdeen and possibly soon in your neighborhood grocery store.

MERLIN
IN DISGUISE

There are folks who swear Bryan Voltaggio can conjure mouth-watering, tummy-happy, and visually astonishing food out of thin air. It's almost true. He turned his hometown city of Frederick, in Frederick County, Maryland, into a foodies' delight. People who couldn't snare a reservation at his famed Volt restaurant needed someplace else to go, and chefs started filling that need. He's brought this magic to Baltimore with an Italian restaurant (in a city known for its Italian restaurants). Focusing on pastas, the menu is seasonal and relies on local farmers. Those of a "certain age" will love the background music based on tunes from the Rat Pack days and cocktails named for Joey Bishop, Peter Lawford, and Sammy Davis Jr. If you liked Bryan (and his California brother Michael) as they competed as finalists in Season 6 of *Top Chef,* you'll love what he's accomplished since then. Yes, cute—restaurant in Frederick is Volt; restaurant in Baltimore is Aggio. Put them together.

Aggio, 614 Water St.
410-528-0200, volt-aggio.com

SNO-BALL'S CHANCE
IN SUMMER

A Baltimore snoball (or snowball or sno-ball) is primarily a seasonal thing. Somewhere around the first day of spring, boards or awnings that had protected the screened openings with lift-up windows from the ravages of winter suddenly disappear. The grinding noises of machines spewing crushed ice awaken. People, from two on up, willingly stand in line for a cup or cone of ice drowned in their favorite flavored syrup—some stands have as many as 150—and realize it was worth waiting for winter to end. The traditional flavor is egg cream topped with marshmallow fluff. The long-time favorite stands are:

B & B Snowballs, 7193 Baltimore Annapolis Blvd.
Glen Burnie (Ferndale)
410 761-0944 Across from the Ferndale Light Rail Station

Icy Delights, 7812 Wise Ave., Dundalk
410 282-2020 Also in Rosedale, Martin Plaza, and Middlesex

One Sweet Moment, 2914 Hamilton Ave.
onesweetmoment.com

SnOasis Snowballs, 30 E Padonia Rd., Lutherville-Timonium
410 666-0537, facebook.com/Snoasis

The Snowball Stand, 1970 Woodstock Rd., Woodstock
facebook.com/thesnowballstand

UNDER THE PINK
FLAMINGO

Although it only opened in 1992, it seems as the Café Hon has been around forever (at least the building is one hundred-plus years old). The center of activity for the Hampden neighborhood, the annual HonFest, and the center of two mini-scandals, one in 2009 because of the large pink flamingo over the entrance and the other in 2010 over whether owner Denise Whiting could trademark the Charm City greeting of "Hon" (she dropped her claim.) Stop by for the house-made pies, food better than your friend's mom makes—we know your Mom's cooking is terrific—and the atmosphere.

Café Hon, 1002 W 36th St., Hampden
410-243-1230, cafehon.com

WHEN YOU WANT TO
CELEBRATE IN STYLE

Somewhat like the Pied Piper of Hamelin, Chef Cindy Wolf opened Charleston in the oh-so-new-again Harbor East area in 1997 and the world followed her. You can choose from three, four, five, or six courses in a prix fixe tasting menu dinner. The award-winning chef adds a French touch to low-country Southern cuisine. It will be different every time, in content, taste, and presentation. Husband Tony Foreman selects the wine list, which usually runs to more than eight hundred bottles from around the world. The waterfront view is almost as delectable as the food. The Foreman-Wolf Restaurant Group also includes Petit Louis, Bin 604 Wine Cellars, Bin 201 Wine Cellars, Pazo, and Cinghiale Osteria.

Charleston, 1000 Lancaster St.
410-332-7373, charlestonrestaurant.com

LEARN HOW TO
ACE YOUR OWN CAKES

Duff Goldman and crew made cake news on the ten seasons of Food Network's *Ace of Cakes* show, which presented them making extraordinary (looking and tasting) cakes for extraordinary occasions. Then, Duff opened Charm City Cakes West on Melrose Avenue in West Hollywood, California, and a new series, *Cake Masters,* showed the L.A. approach to cake design. You don't have to order a cake to try the deliciousness. The shop is open Thursday through Saturday, and you can pick up merchandise, cupcakes, and cake jars (Mason jars with a cake inside). If you've ever thought, "I have an imagination, I could do that. If I had the kitchen, the equipment, the staff, etc.," well, now you can.

Mary Smith, director of class programming for Charm City Cakes, conducts cake-making classes every Saturday, year-round, so you can learn some of their secrets to goodness. They're for people eighteen and older (exception made for adult/child participation). They also have cupcake parties about twice a month and cupcake classes for children ages six through seventeen. Occasionally, Mary Smith, a show regular, conducts a week-long Cake University.

Charm City Bakery, 2936 Remington Ave.
410-235-9229, charmcitycakes.com

GUTEN
APPITI!

Although enough people of French heritage moved here from Canada's Maritime Provinces (beginning in the mid-1700s) to have an area called Frenchtown (now Seton Hill Historic District), it's a German bakery that causes mouths to water. Started in 1927 by William Hoehn, Hoehn's bakery in Highlandtown is now a second- and third-generation operation. William's granddaughter, Sharon Hoehn Hooper, with her cousin Louis Sahlender, now operates it. Sharon's brother, Bob, does the promotions and special events, and their mom does the bookkeeping. Sharon's husband, Larry Hooper, does the maintenance. They bake from scratch without preservatives and little machinery. The original brick hearth oven is still in use and many recipes came over from Germany with William Hoehn. Ask locals for their favorite and you'll hear a list of everything they sell, including donuts, buns, tarts, crullers, cupcakes, brownies, cakes, bread (Vienna and rye daily and 7 grain on Friday), Danish, eclairs, and, of course, German chocolate cake. That's just a tiny list of the items they make. They also make seasonal offerings (e.g., hot cross buns for Easter). Alas, they do not make special occasion decorated (birthday, anniversary) cakes.

Hoehn's Bakery, 400 S Conkling St.
410-675-2884, hoehnsbakery.com

MANGIARE!

You've had thin-crust pizza and deep-dish pizza, so now it's time to try pizza made with focaccia and other Sicilian-based delicacies in this small, intimate eatery in Little Italy. Everyone raves about the meatballs appetizer, even those who grew up in Italian families. However, the Sicilian stack—mozzarella, tomato, basil, eggplant, and prosciutto drizzled with olive oil and balsamic—holds its own. Enjoy an entrée, but save room for the dessert that is a plate of five cream puffs filled with vanilla cream and coated with hazelnut crumble. This is not a fast-food emporium. Come, sit, talk with Joe, the servers, the other guests, have a panini or a Sicilian-style pizza, and enjoy.

Joe Benny's Focacceria, 313 S High St.
443-835-4866, joebennys.com

NO BETTER WAY
TO BREAK THE FAST

There's an art to breakfast and Miss Shirley's has been mastering it since 2005, although it seems as though she's been around forever. Now at three locations (its first location was in Roland Park), this award-winning eatery offers such tastiness as raspberry white chocolate waffles, banana pancakes, coconut cream-stuffed French toast, shrimp and grits, chicken and waffles, and crab cake and fried green tomato eggs Benedict. There's always a seasonal touch on the menu, as in the fall specials of oysters Benedict, the Mac Crabby (jumbo lump crab meat, five cheeses, tomatoes, jalapeno-smoked bacon, and roasted corn), and broccoli salad. Oh, and "Miss Shirley" is restaurateur Eddie Dopkin's tribute to a friend, Shirley McDowell, another food professional. Miss Shirley's is open for breakfast and lunch.

Miss Shirley's Café, 513 W Cold Spring Ln., 410-528-5272
750 E Pratt St., 410-528-5373
1 Park Pl., Annapolis, 410-268-5171
missshirleys.com

FOOD HALL MEETS
Y'ALL COME

Baltimore has had food markets forever (see the Shopping and Fashion section) so it's interesting to see this "new" concept—more than a food court, less than a bunch of restaurants—take so many people by surprise. At the Mt. Vernon Marketplace, you can choose from oysters, dumplings, cheese and meat plates, crepes, soups, olive oils, and beer. There are numerous restaurants and shops, so everyone is sure to find something to please the palate. What was once a department store where you could buy just about everything you needed, all in different departments, is now a different kind of department store focusing on food and drink. There's The Local Oyster, Pinch Dumplings, Cultured Charcuterie, Taps Fill Station, Edible Favors, Ful Café, Micha's Sorbet, The Tomboy Shop, Between 2 Buns, Delights by Mina, Brown Rice, Eat Taste Love, Ceremony Coffee, Big Bean Theory, and Fresh Mondays. Eat in or take home (pretend you slaved all day?).

Mount Vernon Marketplace, 520 Park Ave.
443-796-7392, mountvernonmarketplace.com

EAST MEETS WEST

Baltimore is often portrayed as the poor stepsister to Washington, D.C., yet Baltimore has a Roy's and D.C. doesn't. In fact, of the twenty Roy's restaurants on the mainland, this is the only one on the East Coast north of Florida! This location of the Hawaiian or Asian fusion restaurant from Hawaii by Chef Roy Yamaguchi has about 50 percent Roy's recipes and 50 percent from our own local chef, Matt Ellis. They offer such special holiday items and drinks as macadamia nut pancakes topped with caramel bananas for Mother's Day brunch, lobster and shrimp omelets, or a "Hulaween" bash. The must-try (at least for dessert) is the melting hot chocolate soufflé (flourless chocolate cake). Order it before your meal because they are made to order. Watch what happens in their signature exhibition kitchen, and stay for Aloha Hour in the bar.

Roy's Restaurant, 720 Aliceanna St.
410-659-0099, roysrestaurant.com/locations/md/baltimore

DELIZIOSO

Wandering around Little Italy is a wonderful assault on your olfactory senses. You stop here to try the pizza or there to try the pasta. Then, it's off to Vaccaro's for di dolci, the sweets or dessert. Actually, they say, and I agree, "Life's short, eat dessert first." They must be doing something right because they've been in business since 1956. They sell Italian cookies, cakes, ricotta cookies, tiramisu and gelato, cannoli (they had a sixty-cent special for large cannoli during their sixtieth anniversary year), rum cake, paninis, mufalato, salad, soups, and so much more. By the way, you can buy the cannoli, unfilled, with a tub of filling to take home. Whether you have fond memories of Italy or want to start some, this is the place to visit.

Vaccaro's Italian Pastry Shop, 222 Albemarle St., 410-685-4905,2919
O'Donnell St. O'Donnell Square (Canton), 410-276-4744
118 Shawan Rd. (Hunt Valley), 410-785-9011
696 Baltimore Pike (Bel Air), 410-838-0000
vaccarospastry.com

THERE IS AN ART
AND A SCIENCE TO THIS

This brewpub or microbrewery, open since 1996, occupies an old town house, up and down. Look for such signature beers as Resurrection, an abbey brown ale; Choptank'd, a light and crisp summer drink; Beazly, Belgian in origin; and Birdhouse, a pale ale. Regular seasonal beers are highlighted along with something new and interesting. Specials are frequent, including a Wednesday night prix fixe summer beer dinner that includes three courses paired with ten-ounce Brewer's Art beers. The normal menu includes small plates and salads, soups, cheeses, entrees, and desserts. The bar food menu is not available in the dining room. Although many items are made with beer, there should be enough items without it to satisfy you. Also, they have a number of vegetarian items. The bar list includes Scotches, whiskeys, and other spirits and wines. They provide funds for numerous city charities, from the Jones Falls Watershed Association to the Women Entrepreneurs of Baltimore to the campaign to fund a second Mr. Trashwheel to help keep the Inner Harbor clean. Brewery tours are offered on Saturday, but not too frequently in the summer.

Brewer's Art, 1106 N Charles St.
410-547-6925, thebrewersart.com

GIVE THANKS
WHERE IT'S DUE

When you give praise to the brewpub and the microbrewery scene in Maryland, you're giving thanks to Hugh Sisson, founder of Clipper City Brewing Company in 1995. He was instrumental in having legislation enacted in Maryland that enabled the creation of the brewpub. In 1994, he left the eponymous Sisson's Brewpub and decided to start his new venture in Baltimore to replace National Bohemian, which had left the state for southern climes. The Clipper City brand name is in honor of the clipper ship, a mainstay of early Baltimore shipbuilding. As Sisson aimed for a wider market, he changed the beer to Heavy Seas, now distributed in eighteen states. Heavy Seas has garnered numerous well-deserved honors. You're invited to take the forty-five-minute tour with beer sampling (must be twenty-one to drink, but the tour is open to all) that starts before the tour, rather than following it, so be early. Call to reserve your spot. Heavy Seas gastropubs are located at 1300 Bank Street, Baltimore, and 1501 Wilson Boulevard, Arlington, Virginia.

Heavy Seas Beer, 4615 Hollins Ferry Rd.
410-247-7822, hsbeer.com

YOU NEVER KNOW
WHAT'S BREWING NEXT

Oliver Breweries is another early 1990s creation, starting in a Baltimore brewpub basement on W. Pratt Street in 1993. The original equipment came from the United Kingdom, and the thought was to brew authentic English ales. They say they've made hundreds of beers since then and are thrilled that they've moved into a larger space that will allow them to can their beer for wider distribution. Among their more famous (or infamous) beers are Modern Life is Rubbish Victorian Porter, Riding Easy Hoppy Blonde Ale, Irish Red Ale, Dark Horse English Dark Mild, Coventry Cream English Bitter, and Ironman English Pale Ale. Seasonal brews are created, with raspberries or cherry blossoms used in spring mixtures. The summer Golden Glory has ginger root and lemongrass in it, and the Harvest Ale has local wild flower honey for a smooth finish. Call or write for tour and tasting information.

Oliver Brewing Company, 4216 Shannon Dr.
410-483-3302, oliverbrewingco.com

EVERMORE,
NOT NEVERMORE

Baltimore's newest and largest brewery, located on the site of Old Oriole Park (before Memorial Stadium), is an incubator for independent craft beers. Peabody Heights Brewery brews the beer for Raven Beer, Monument City, Full Tilt, Fin City, and Antietam Brewing. They also brew thirty different types of their own beer, with some regular tastes and some experimental brews. You can stop by their tasting room to try one of the fifteen beers on draft. They host numerous events, many open to the public, including Pints and Poses, where you can take a free hour-long yoga class (donations to the month's charity are appreciated) followed by a cash bar. They also have trivia nights, square dancing, a crab feast, a winter film series, food trucks or caterers on Friday night, and the occasional Sri Lankan beer pairing dinner. Tours are offered on a regular basis.

Peabody Heights Brewery, 401 E 30th St.
410-467-7837, peabodyheightsbrewery.com

YOUR NEIGHBORHOOD BEER OPERATION

Open to the public Thursday through Saturday, Union Craft takes community participation to a high level. In May 2016, they collaborated with local filmmakers Jeff Krulik and John Heyn in celebrating the thirtieth anniversary of their cult film, *Heavy Metal Parking Lot* (about the parking lot activities before a Judas Priest concert at the old Capital Centre arena in suburban Maryland on May 31, 1986), by issuing an HMPL Belgian-style Strong Golden Ale. It was packaged in kegs and sixteen-ounce tall-boy cans (no bottles for any Union Craft brews). Alex Fine, a Baltimore illustrator, designed the can's artwork. They produce a number of beers, with Anthem, Duckpin, Double Duckpin, Steady Eddie, and others as regular fare and seasonal flavors as appropriate. You can order a beer or a flight or create your own flight. Outdoor seating is available weather permitting. There's usually a food truck outside on Saturday or you can order from nearby restaurants, and often there's music. Brewery tours are conducted on Saturday, starting about every hour on the half-hour. And, you can play cornhole, at least before you've had too many brews. Oh, it's next to the Woodberry Light Rail stop.

Union Craft Brewing Company, 1700 Union Ave.
410-467-0290, unioncraftbrewing.com

IF IT'S ADVERTISED ON NATIONAL TV,
IT PROBABLY ISN'T HERE

One reason for visiting Alewife is to try some or all of the forty beers they have on draft, including a couple of local brews that range from $6.50 to $12 for a glass that's twelve or sixteen ounces. There's also who-knows-how-many different bottled beers from around the country and the planet that range from $7 to $30 for bottles that go from twelve to thirty ounces. They aim to be a great craft beer spot, and they succeed. Never fear if you aren't a beer drinker. Alewife has numerous house cocktails that are made with "selected ingredients including house made syrups, mixers, and purees." The food menu includes several appetizers, small bites and sandwiches, and some entrees available from 4 to 10 p.m. The menu changes occasionally, but relies on locally sourced products. There are also trivia challenges. It's convenient to the Hippodrome and Everyman Theatre and not that far from the Convention Center or Camden Yards, so it's convenient for a before-show/game meal.

Alewife, 21 N Eutaw St.
410-545-5112, alewifebaltimore.com

NOTHING TO BEEF
ABOUT HERE

At one time, enough Jewish delicatessens lined Lombard Street near the Lloyd Street Synagogue to earn the name Corned Beef Row. The oldest is The Original Attman's Deli, Authentic New York Delicatessen, since 1915. It's operated by third-generation Marc Attman. Whether you come for the atmosphere or the corned beef, pastrami, half-done pickles, Ida's Jewish Apple cake, and Dr. Brown's soda, you connect to the community's history. This is kosher-style deli, not a kosher one, for they also sell corned beef and Swiss, baked ham, and shrimp salad. Tables for forty-two people are in the Kibbitz Room.

Attman's Deli, 1019 E Lombard Street, Jonestown
(also in Cabin John, Montgomery County)
410-563-2666, baltimore.attmansdeli.com

THEY TRAINED THEM RIGHT

Just to the right of the entrance to the Kimpton's Monaco Hotel, in a historic Beaux-Arts building that was once the Baltimore and Ohio Railroad headquarters, is the B&O American Brasserie. You can find a superb meal here that's perfect for a special occasion or a business meeting. More important, you can find some equally splendid mixed drinks. Stop by for happy hour, try a locally brewed beer on tap (including Union Craft "Duck Pin"), or taste a bottled or canned beer from around the state and the planet or something from their wine list. If you want a cocktail, try the Queen Bee (Grey Goose vodka, yuzu, St. Elder, and honey syrup), the Cat's Pajamas (Barr Hill Tom Cat gin, lemon, Bärenjäger, rhubarb spirit, and Millstone hopvine cider), or a B&O Old Fashioned (George Dickel rye, Abbott's bitters, Amaro Nonino, crème de cacao, and Laphroig). Spending the night in the hotel? Try a Glenmorangie flight of three Glenmorangie cask-finished whiskeys. And, if for some reason, you can't find anything you want on the menu, ask the bartender to fix something you'd like.

B&O American Brasserie, 2 N Charles St.
443-692-6172, bandorestaurant.com

THERE'S A REASON
IT'S CALLED A TAPHOUSE

Where to start on this Fells Point pub? Monday Sucks Happy Hour features one dollar off almost all drafts all day; Tuesday beer social lets you sample rare and exotic beers at special prices and hear a guest speaker; at Wednesday pinch-the-pint night, you keep the souvenir glass; play Thursday Charm City Trivia upstairs in the Mobtown Lounge; or enjoy Friday Big Ass Draft Happy Hour, when most thirty-two-ounce draft is just seven dollars. Expect more than one thousand bottles, 102 taps, five casks, three separate bars, and crowds, particularly on weekends, a decent food menu that's not too complex and not too "typical bar food," and enough TV sets for serious sports fans. They've been pouring beer since 1988 and are doing something right. Frequent events include an Annual Belgian Beer Fest, Rare & Obscure, Hopfest, American Craft Beer Week, Italian Fest, and brewery-specific events so you can taste new beers and meet beer experts.

Max's Taphouse, 735 S Broadway
410-675-6297, maxs.com

A MODERN AMERICAN TAVERN
BY MICHAEL MINA

Okay, start with the Michael Mina thing. Add the location—inside the Four Seasons Hotel and a waterfront view (outdoor dining when weather permits)—and you know this is where you want to stop for that special occasion. Whatever food and beverage trend you're following, Wit & Wisdom probably created it or has been there, done that, and gone on to something newer. That's not their only claim to fame, though, when it comes to potables. If you want the news on wines, join sommelier Julie Dalton for her once-a-month, two-hour "interactive, fun, and approachable way to sip, swirl, and learn about the wonderful world of wine! Enjoy multiple tastings and delectable snacks from Chef Zack Mills." Topics include A Toast to Summer, A Tribute to France, Perfect Turkey Wine, and Bubbles (champagne). Class is limited to twenty-four participants and reservations are required.

Wit & Wisdom, 200 International Dr.
410-576-5800, witandwisdomtavern.com

MUSIC AND ENTERTAINMENT

CURTAIN UP!

While the nation's perception of Baltimore's professional theatrical scene has had its ups and downs, Arena Players has shown its merit. It's the longest continuously operating African American community theater in the country. With ambitious and well-executed seasons that present musicals, comedies, dramas, revivals, and new works, it has a loyal following that's kept it going since 1953. The company looks to the community to cast its six productions (open call for the season is usually in July). Its Youtheatre program, for children ages four through eighteen, gives youngsters a chance to learn drama, music, dance, and theater production. The Studio 801 program does the same for adults who want to perform and learn about the theater. You, too, can be a star—performer, painter, designer . . . who knows?

Arena Players, 801 McCulloh St.
410-728-6500, arenaplayersinc.com

TIME TO BEAT
THE BAND

From its inception in 1915 through today and a bunch of tomorrows, the extraordinary and world-renowned Baltimore Symphony Orchestra has been an integral part of the city and beyond. Its list of "firsts" includes the nation's first orchestra to offer a concert series for children in 1924; the 2005 naming of Marin Alsop as Music Director, the first female music director of a major American symphony orchestra; and the 2008 creation of OrchKids for children. You can hear the BSO at the Joseph Meyerhoff Symphony Hall and other venues.

Baltimore Symphony Orchestra, 1212 Cathedral St.
410-783-8000, bsomusic.org

THERE AREN'T EVEN SMALL ACTORS
ON THIS SCREEN

Once, there were four thousand drive-in movie theaters (there are 336 as of 2016) and Maryland had forty-two. Bengies Drive-In Theatre, which opened June 6, 1956 in Middle River, is the only one remaining in Maryland. However, it does boast the biggest screen—fifty-two feet high by 120 feet wide—in the country. It's considered a Maryland state "treasure." Showing movies from late spring through fall, D. Edward Vogel, the owner of Bengies, says the shows, both current and classics, generally start with a film rated G, PG, or PG-13. A second film follows that, and on weekends, there's often a third film.

Bengies, 3417 Eastern Blvd., Middle River
410-687-5627, bengies.com

YOU WANT TO THROW
THE WORD ECLECTIC
IN THERE SOMEPLACE

A couple of historic Beaux-Arts buildings are home to the Charles Theatre, which isn't terribly historic but feels as though it should be. It shows first-run specialty films, indies, Hollywood movies, foreign films, and cinema classics on its five screens. It has cachet and is artsy without really trying. You just know that whatever you're seeing there is special and you're going to feel good having seen it. They have an anime series, a Cinema Sundays at the Charles Theatre with bagels and a Q&A, a revival series, and performances of the Metropolitan Opera. It's everything a neighborhood theater should be.

Charles Theatre, 1711 N Charles St.
410-727-3456, thecharles.com

AND BUBBLE
YOUR TROUBLE AWAY

Bromo-Seltzer was a brand of antacid (and hangover cure) invented by Captain Isaac Emerson in 1888. This building was constructed in 1911 and, at 289 feet and fifteen stories tall, it was the tallest building in the city until 1923. Inspired by the Palazzo Vecchio in Florence, Italy, it has a four-dial gravity clock with the Bromo-Seltzer letters replacing the numbers. At the tower's top, it had a twenty-ton, rotating, fifty-one-foot blue steel replica Bromo bottle that was used as a guide for returning sailors who could see it from as far as twenty miles away. The armature rusted and the bottle was removed in 1936. The building fell into disrepair and was threatened with demolition. Fortunately, philanthropists Eddie and Sylvia Brown funded the tower's restoration. Now home to more than thirty painters, jewelers, writers, digital artists, and performers, there's an open house every Saturday from 11 a.m. to 4 p.m., and clock room tours are offered for a fee. The elevator goes to the fifteenth floor, then there's a flight of steps that leads to a ship's ladder to climb to the top. The clock is being restored and should be complete before the end of 2016.

Bromo-Seltzer Arts Tower, 21 S Eutaw St.
443-874-3596, bromoseltzertower.com

ACRES AND ACRES
OF NON-CITY LIFE

When you want to escape the city, you can head to the Mt. Washington Arboretum and take a walk around the pond. At an acre, it's tiny and manageable for a quick break. When you want something more substantial, head to the 207-acre Cylburn Arboretum, the city's largest public garden. You can even reach this place on the Jones Falls Trail from the Inner Harbor for when you want to make a full day's nature outing. The buildings and grounds have a history that dates from the mid-1800s. You can wander through trees and twenty gardens replete with azaleas, bamboo, beeches, boxwoods, chestnuts, conifers, hollies, Japanese maples, magnolias, oaks, and other flora. A nature museum shows Maryland birds, butterflies, rocks and minerals, and more. You can hike three-and-a-half miles of trails, go birding, visit the aquaponics project, and participate in the numerous regularly scheduled activities—all within a long stone's throw of Charm City center. Oh, and your dog, on a leash, is welcome.

Cylburn Arboretum, 4915 Greenspring Ave.
410-367-2217, cylburnassocation.org

MEMORIES OF YOU

Easily one of the lesser-known attractions and performance venues in Baltimore, the James "Eubie" Blake Cultural Center pays tribute to this American composer, lyricist, and pianist of ragtime, jazz, and popular music. Although he lived from 1887 to 1983, if you follow the Broadway stage scene, you should have heard of the 1978 musical *Eubie!*, which featured his works, and the more recent sort-of-revival of his *Shuffle Along*. One of the first Broadway musicals, it debuted this time around at the Music Box Theatre in April 2016 as *Shuffle Along, Or the Making of the Musical Sensation of 1921 and All That Followed*. It was considered a new show rather than a revival and thus didn't win any of its ten Tony nominations. Eubie was born in Baltimore, and he and his wife Marion were convinced to donate his memorabilia to the Maryland Historical Society. The center honors other Baltimore jazz greats including Cab Calloway, Billie Holiday, Chick Webb, and Avon Long. Joyous music from live performances fills the building, and it has fascinating, informative, and entertaining events, programs, and activities.

Eubie Blake Cultural Center, 847 N Howard St.
410-225-3130, eubieblake.org

LIFE
UPON THE WICKED STAGE

While some mourned the closing of the Morris Mechanic Theatre in 2004, the facility with its capacity for 1,614 people was too small to support many traveling Broadway shows and too big to be affordable. However, the Everyman Theatre, just a few blocks away in the Bromo Arts and Entertainment District, has been around since 1990, providing exciting and extraordinary professional performances of classic and newer shows, in an intimate, 253-seat setting. Starting with one production a year, they now offer a half-dozen shows and other programming in a building with as interesting a past as the shows they perform. The regional theater has a resident company with auditions for Equity and non-Equity performers, usually in May. They also provide opportunities to learn about the theater for high school students and acting classes for all ages.

Everyman Theatre, 315 W Fayette St.
410-752-2208, everymantheatre.org

MODERN DAY GEPPETTO

Steve Geppi knows how to pull your nostalgic strings at the eponymous Geppi's Entertainment Museum. The entertaining and educational history of pop culture is told and shown through the huge collection—most of it Geppi's—of comic books, newspapers, magazines, movies, television paraphernalia, toys, buttons, radio and video game memorabilia, cereal boxes, vintage dolls, Pez dispensers, and entertainment history from the seventeenth century to current times. (Yes, this is the same Steve Geppi who's part owner of the Orioles, publisher of *Baltimore* magazine, and involved in numerous charitable organizations.)

Geppi's Entertainment Museum, 301 W Camden St., Downtown
410-625-7060, geppismuseum.com

WHAT A BLAST!

Fireworks are a regular event for July 4, Labor Day festivities, and at other times in various neighborhoods. The biggest blasts come at the Inner Harbor, though, on July 4 and New Year's Eve. The obvious vantage points are around the Inner Harbor, including Harborplace itself, Federal Hill, Locust Point, Fells Point, Canton, and Harbor East. Join the throngs and go boom! If you don't want to deal with hot and humid or cold and snowy, reserve a room in a nearby hotel. Whether a guest room or public area, the viewing opportunities depend on where the fireworks barges are located. Just ask for a harbor view on an upper floor and hope for the best. Or, head to their viewing spot. Also, some restaurants offer special meals for the events. In either case, reservations should be made as soon as you think about going.

TIP
Festivities for the Fourth generally start about 7 p.m. with live music, with fireworks starting about 9:30. New Year's Eve music starts about 9 p.m. and the fireworks take off at midnight.

Fireworks Inner Harbor
410-752-8632, promotionandarts.org

Baltimore Marriott Waterfront
(not Marriott Inner Harbor)
700 Aliceanna St., 410-385-3000
marriott.com
The fifth-floor observation deck by the pool is best but may be
limited to Marriott Rewards membership or members of a certain
level.

Four Seasons Hotel Baltimore
200 International Dr., 410-576-5800
fourseasons.com/baltimore
Patio in the Wit and Wisdom restaurant.

Hyatt Regency Baltimore Inner Harbor
300 Light St., 410-528-1234
baltimore.hyatt.com
In the pool area on the sixth floor, for hotel guests.

Royal Sonesta Harbor Court Baltimore
550 Light St., 410-234-0550
sonesta.com/baltimore
The Explorer's Lounge restaurant on the second level (hotel guests
and others) or the terrace on the seventh floor (hotel guests only).

Café Gia
410 S High St., 410-685-6727
cafegiabaltimore.com

Rusty Scupper
410-727-3678
rusty-scupper.com

TONIGHT –
THE MOON
HAV–A–LOOK

HAV-A-LOOK!

Asking for my favorite "must-do" Baltimore experience receives a quick and easy answer. Visit Herman Heyn in Fells Point on a clear weekend night. He's set up at the Thames Street end of Broadway Square with an eight-inch Schmidt-Cassegrain reflector telescope so you can see the moon, planets, and stars. He may give you a yellow sticker with a legend, "I Saw Saturn" (or Mars or Jupiter). He's been doing this since November 13, 1987. Even his web site is fun and educational. Magical things can happen when you have a telescope in front of you. Heyn relates the story about a man and a woman in town on business. They came to Fells Point one night and "came across me, and looked at Saturn. A year later the man was back and told me the above story, adding it was a very significant night. Seeing Saturn together inspired a relationship which led to marriage!" Obviously, he doesn't guarantee that will happen every time, but he does guarantee that you'll be amazed and learn something. There's no charge, but "hat" contributions are accepted. Due to weather and other contingencies, please call so you won't be disappointed.

Herman Heyn, Street-Corner Astronomer, Fells Point
410-889-0460, hermanheyn.com

ALL THE WORLD'S A STAGE

Morey Amsterdam, Jack Benny, Milton Berle, Benny Goodman, Bob Hope, Martha Raye, Dinah Shore, Red Skelton, the Three Stooges, the Andrews Sisters, and Frank Sinatra with Harry James all performed at the Hippodrome Theatre during the 1930s. If those names don't mean anything to you, ask your parents or grandparents. It was the largest theater south of Philadelphia and home for vaudeville performers, movies, the premieres of several Broadway-bound shows, and road companies of Broadway shows. When it closed in 1990, it was the last movie theater in the downtown area. A major 2004 renovation has brought new life to the venue that presents Broadway road shows, concerts, and other attractions. Monday morning behind-the-scenes tours, Camp Hippodrome, Young Critics, and Master Classes are just a few of the other programs at the Performing Arts Center.

Hippodrome at France-Merrick Performing Arts Center, 12 N Eutaw St. 410-547-7328, france-merrickpac.com/index.php

NO SCROOGES ALLOWED

Millions of people have had their hearts brightened by the uncountable number of lights displayed on the homes in Hampden every December. The residents of the 700 block of 34th Street have created the Miracle on 34th Street, a display of holiday lights and other decorations that draws visitors from around the world. Between Keswick Road and Chestnut Avenue, you're likely to see Santas, Christmas trees made of hubcaps, trains, pink flamingos, a Chanukah menorah, snowmen made of bicycle wheels, and other symbols of winter and the holiday spirit. A spontaneous caroling may erupt. On the first Sunday of December, the Mayor's Christmas Parade marches down two-and-a-half miles of Hampden streets with 160 marching units, floats, local personalities, one hundred-plus Harley-Davidson motorcycles, bands, Philadelphia Mummers, and, always, a jolly Santa. The parade route comes down Falls Road to 36th Street (the "Avenue"), heads north on Chestnut Avenue, and ends at 37th Street.

Miracle on 34th Street, 720 W 34th St.
christmasstreet.com

OPERA, ROCK,
BALLROOM, AND MORE

The historic Lyric Opera House, or The Lyric, was renamed the Patricia & Arthur Modell Performing Arts Center at The Lyric in 2010, with thanks for the $3.5 million gift from the former Baltimore Ravens owner and his wife. A variety of live entertainment is presented, including Yanni, Maks and Val: Our Way, Baltimore Grand Prix & Fitness Expo Pre-Judging, Chris Tucker, Kathleen Madigan, Peter Frampton, Blue Man Group, and full-stage operatic performances with English surtitles. The Peabody at the Lyric combines traditional opera and American musical theater for extraordinary shows by tomorrow's stars. Other activities, including "Opera-To-Go" and "Opera Cares," are presented in schools and community centers. Tours that explore the history, architecture, and culture of the performing arts center, from the stage-house to the box office (and where *House of Cards* was shot) are among the highlights.

Modell Performing Arts Center, 140 W Mt. Royal Ave.
410-900-1150, lyricbaltimore.com

YOU CAN SEE OUT
BUT THEY CAN'T SEE IN

Drive through and around Baltimore, particularly Highlandtown, on a summer's day and you'll most likely see window and door screens with idyllic paintings of rambling brooks, a stand of woods, or other pastoral scenes, with an occasional abstract image or two thrown in. This is a tradition that dates from 1913 and is unique to Baltimore. Screens are "canvasses with holes" to let summer breezes in without nosy neighbors seeing you in your all-together. Learn how to create your own screen by joining a class or organize a private painting party. You can commission your own painted screen. Seminars, workshops, and other public events are scheduled throughout the year. Tours are available. For more information on painted screens, visit the online shop for a documentary film or a brochure about the Painted Screens Pilgrimage or buy Elaine Eff's book *The Painted Screens of Baltimore: An Urban Folk Art Revealed.*

Painted Screens Society
paintedscreens@verizon.net
paintedscreens.org

TRYING FOR CLARITY
IN MENTAL HEALTH

When you want some context to Baltimore, Enoch Pratt, Moses Sheppard, and most important, the history of mental health care at Sheppard Pratt, this is the place to visit. Focusing on removing the stigma of mental illness, art works by local, national, and internationally renowned artists are in the museum and on the walls throughout the hospital. Each has or was impacted in some way by mental illness or addiction. More than two thousand artifacts—books, documents, furniture, photographs, artwork, equipment, and assorted memorabilia—belonged to Moses Sheppard, the founder. There's also an exhibit on Enoch Pratt and the hospital's early years. The museum is named in honor of Robert Gibson, a former Sheppard Pratt president, and his wife in honor of his 32 years of service to the health system. The museum is open by appointment.

Robert and Diane Gibson Museum, 6501 N Charles St.
443-286-5626, sheppardpratt.org

CURTAIN UP!

The now-iconic Senator opened in 1939 and thrived, barely survived, didn't, and now is thriving again. It has a main auditorium, two private screening rooms, and three new, smaller, more intimate theaters. Theatre 2 holds 160 and features a forty-foot curved screen, Theatre 3 holds sixty, and Theatre 4 seats fifty-seven. The Art Deco design has been retained and is worth the visit just to explore the architecture and décor. Look for glass blocks, murals, the original terrazzo floors in the lobby, and the impressive gold curtain in the main theater that still opens prior to the movie presentation. The Senator is on the U.S. National Register of Historic Places and was the first theater to receive a Historic Cinema Certification. Beyond that, of course, are the movies they show. You'll see first-runs and revivals—some recent examples include *Koyaanisqatsi, Blazing Saddles,* and *Jaws* 3-D and regular—and in-between. Dolby Digital sound and digital projection mean this old theater is just as good as new, only better. Barry Levinson and John Waters have held premieres here, and there's a Walk of Fame in the sidewalk.

Senator Theatre, 5904 York Rd.
410-323-4424, thesenatortheatre.com

TO INFINITY
AND BEYOND . . .

Once you've met Herman Heyn (Baltimore's Street-Corner Astronomer) and caught the astronomy bug, it's time to move on to this place. This science center, on the Johns Hopkins University campus, operates the science program for the Hubble Space Telescope and conducts the science and mission operations for the James Webb Space Telescope. It also supports other astronomy programs and conducts research. Right here in Baltimore! But, back to you. As the Institute people say, if you're interested in "planets, stars, galaxies, and black holes," then their free public lectures are for you. Attend in person or watch online. A noted scientist discusses a different cosmic topic the first Tuesday of every month. Topics might be: Planetary Tales from the Stellar Crypt: Exoplanets Surviving the Death of their Host Star; Why We Need to Understand Stars to Find The Next Earth; or On the Trail of the Missing Galaxies: The Oldest Stars in the Neighborhood. Lectures start at 8 p.m.

Space Telescope Science Institute, 3700 San Martin Dr.
410-338-4973, stsci.edu/portal

TRANQUIL CENTERING

Years ago, before the Birds moved from Memorial Stadium to Camden Yards, they occupied some hallowed ground on 33rd Street. They moved. They stadium was no more. Stadium Place was built, where people live and play now. As of 2004, a Santa Rosa-style blue flagstone labyrinth, surrounded by gardens and an interfaith pavilion, welcomes visitors to Stadium Place. Of the fifteen labyrinths in Baltimore, some are private, some are located on church grounds. This one, at sixty-five feet, is one of the largest. You don't need complex instructions to benefit from walking a labyrinth. The instructions are simple. Leave your cares and worries at the entrance. No talking. Concentrate on your breathing. Follow the path to the center. Stand there for a moment or two, if you wish, and then retrace your steps. A labyrinth's beauty is the limited choices you have, the speed at which you walk, whether you stop along the way, and when you return. You can't make any wrong turns. The walk is seen as a way of releasing daily stress.

Stadium Place – Thanksgiving Labyrinth, 1000 E 33rd St.
410-433-2442 ext. 15, naturesacred.org/sacred_places/stadium-place-2

SPORTS AND RECREATION

CAMERA, LIGHTS, ACTION

Budding or frustrated filmmakers gather every year to participate in the Baltimore version of the 48 Hour Film Project that spans 153 cities in six continents. Gather a group of volunteers who write, cast, produce, rehearse, costume, sound, edit, and output to tape or other media to create a film that's between four and seven minutes long. Easy, you think. Just do everything in advance. No such luck. Bob Hatch, Baltimore producer, announces a kick-off date. Everyone gathers and your team picks two genres from a hat (for example, musical, coming of age, romance, or Western) and chooses which one you'll use. Hatch tells you a character, a prop, and a line of dialogue must be included. That could be Pat Dobson, arborist, a banana, and "It works for me." And, off you go. The films are screened, judged, and voted on, with awards presented to outstanding performers and other highlights (a mini-Oscar celebration).

The winner of Best Film will go on to represent Baltimore as it vies for Best Film of the World against 152 other city winners at Filmapalooza 2017 and an opportunity to screen at the Cannes Film Festival 2017, Court Métrage (short film).

Baltimore 48HFP, PO Box 40008, Washington, DC
48hourfilm.com/baltimore

YOU KNOW YOU CAN,
YOU KNOW YOU CAN

The difference, as we know, between men and boys (and girls) is the price of their toys. You don't want to know how much the "toys" cost here, but you can dream big. This historic national landmark, the birthplace of American railroading, has the oldest and most comprehensive American railroad collection in the world! Yes, they're still collecting. It has humongous trains, little trains—an outdoor G-scale layout and an indoor HO scale model—toy trains, trains to climb, and trains to ride. Nearly two hundred pieces of locomotives and rolling stock, from 1830 through today, fill the enormous property. The roundhouse answers a question some people never asked—how did engines change direction or come in for maintenance? For the truly young, there's a kids zone, toddler time, and a train carousel. You can only begin to imagine the toys, apparel, books, and souvenirs for sale in the gift shop.

B&O Railroad Museum, 901 W Pratt St.
410-752-2490, borail.org

A LONG FLY BALL
FROM CAMDEN YARDS

Only three blocks west of Camden Yards is the George "Babe" Herman Ruth birthplace and museum. To get there, start at the statue of Babe Ruth—with the wrong-handed glove on his hip—at the stadium and follow the sixty baseballs on the sidewalk that lead to his home (and the three adjacent homes). Yes, it's all things Babe Ruth and baseball. It's much more intimate and creative than the one in Cooperstown, New York, and, after a 2015 rehabilitation, it's ADA compliant. My favorite memory is a wedding with a recessional under raised bats. Entrance is now on Dover Street.

Babe Ruth Birthplace and Museum, 216 Emory St.
410-727-1539, baberuthmuseum.org

CHOO-CHOO

Once you've seen the real trains, it's time to see a smaller version. The BSME club has two twelve-by-sixty-five-foot HO and O scale two-rail model train layouts. If that means something to you, then you definitely want to visit. If it's Greek to you, then you definitely want to visit. You'll see model steam and diesel trains, interurbans, and trolleys running off an overhead wire. You're sure to learn a lot because trains and models have changed since the five-car Lionel train set you had when you were seven years old. At 2,500 square feet, that's not so miniature, though. The freight and passengers trains pass through a large city, rolling countryside, and small towns meant to remind you of the Eastern Appalachian region of the United States. Formed in 1932, the BSME has the largest permanent display in the mid-Atlantic area. They have an open house every Sunday in January, the second Sunday of each month except May, and much more during the winter holiday season. You're expected to ooh, ah, and ask lots of questions.

Baltimore Society of Model Engineers, 225 W Saratoga St.
410-837-3763, modelengineers.com

CREEPY CRAWLY
CRITTERS

Tucked away in Leakin Park is the Carrie Murray Nature Center, housing an insect zoo and a rehab center for disabled birds of prey. It's named for the mother of former Baltimore Orioles' first baseman and Hall of Famer Eddie Murray (#33). Explore nature and learn about the thousands of animals and insects native to this area. Programs last from a couple of hours to week-long summer camps focusing on conservation, arts and crafts, and multicultural studies. Attend a full-moon owl prowl, summer solstice celebration, mad scientist session, great bug hunt, nature scavenger hunt, hay ride, or hike. Among the birds of prey inhabiting the center are owls, hawks, vultures, and a falcon. All the birds (except one owl) are natives. Eighty-five percent have been hit by cars on busy highways. People throw food out the window, thinking it's biodegradable, then a squirrel comes along to investigate, then the bird of prey thinks, "there's a juicy meal," swoops down, and smack. If they're lucky, they become permanent non-releasable residents of the center and they're used in educational programming.

Carrie Murray Nature Center, 1901 Ridgetop Rd.
410-396-0808, carriemurraynaturecenter.org

YOU DON'T HAVE
TO JOIN THE NAVY

Boating is synonymous with Baltimore. The first trip is via the water taxi that makes a dozen stops around the Inner Harbor. When you're ready to travel farther, hop aboard one of two cruise ships, Carnival's *Pride* or Royal Caribbean's *Grandeur of the Sea,* that sail year-round from the port, cruising to the Caribbean, Bermuda, New England, and Canada. Other ships also stop at Charm City. It's within a six-hour drive of 40 million people, so it's easy to understand why more than 240,000 people choose the city for their departure point.

Baltimore Water Taxi, 1800 S Clinton St.
410-563-3900, baltimorewatertaxi.com

American Cruise Lines
800-460-4518, americancruiselines.com

Carnival Cruise Lines
800-764-7419, carnival.com

Crystal Cruises
888-722-0021, crystalcruises.com/luxury-cruises

Royal Caribbean Cruise Lines
866-562-7625, royalcaribbean.com

SOFTLY WE GLIDE

Think of a nice, sentimental movie that takes place in the winter, and there's almost certainly a scene at an ice rink—people flirting with each other, parents teaching children the basics, others practicing leaps and spins, or dreaming of winning the gold at an upcoming Winter Olympics. Baltimore doesn't have a Rockefeller Center ice rink, but it does have the Pandora rink. It's small, but it's an ice rink in a great location, at the intersection of Pratt and Light Streets. The Inner Harbor has had winter ice skating at Rash Field off and on since the late 1980s. There's hope that it will be returned there (for one, it would be a normal size rink). Until then, there's the Pandora rink.

Pandora Ice Rink, 201 E Pratt St.
410-779-4700 ext. 5308, innerharboricerink.org

Mimi DiPietro Family Skating Center
Patterson Park, 200 S Linwood Ave.
410-396-9392, pattersonpark.com/skating/skating.html

LIONS, CHEETAHS, PENGUINS, AND GIRAFFES,
OH, MY

You've seen this zoo, formerly known as the Baltimore Zoo and the Baltimore City Zoo, or some other zoo, with its more-than-160-acre facility in beautiful Druid Hill Park. Admire the changes they've made over the years—it is the country's third-oldest zoo, dating from 1836—grab a bite to eat, and enjoy. It's the specials that are, well, special. There's a penguin encounter at the new Penguin Coast exhibit, where you can have a photo op with a penguin, or breakfast with the animals, take an animal craft safari, enjoy a sip and stroll, spend overnights at the zoo, and much more. Or, with a fee of at least three hundred dollars for four people, have a behind-the-scenes encounter. It's like watching a special on the National Geographic or Smithsonian cable channel except you're right there with the show's stars. You choose from five itineraries (giraffe and okapi, rhino, zebra and ostrich, penguin, and polar bear), according to your interests, or make a day of it and take all five.

Maryland Zoo in Baltimore, Druid Hill Park
410-396-7102, marylandzoo.org

ONCE MORE,
NOT NEVERMORE

The Ravens have excited and disappointed us over the years, but the good is better than the bad. Super Bowl champions in 2000 and 2012 is nothing to caw at. There's more to M&T Bank Stadium than a game or a concert, though. Groups of twenty or more (five dollars a person) or less (one hundred dollars for one through nineteen people) can take the ninety-minute walking tour behind the scenes and get partial access onto the field, into the locker room, into the seating bowl, onto the club suite level, and into the press box. Learn about some of what it takes to prepare everything for the teams or performers, guests, food, beverages, and media coverage. It's a lot more than having the gang over for some brews and pizza.

M&T Bank Stadium, 1101 Russell St., 410-261-7283
baltimoreravens.com/gameday/mt-bank-stadium/stadium-tours.html

TIP

at least five days in advance for tours
ed Tuesday, Wednesday, Thursday
ternoon) and Saturday. Tour groups
receive free parking in lot D (enter at Gate F).

ON YOUR MARK

Baltimore has more than its share of athletic heroes, particularly football and baseball. We also have swimmer Michael Phelps, the winningest Olympian ever. It's unlikely that anyone will ever duplicate his accomplishments. You and I can't be the next Phelps, but we can swim where he swam. Join the Meadowbrook Aquatic and Fitness Center (or make friends with an existing member) and swim during open swim time. By the way, the indoor and outdoor lap pools are fifty meters. If you're used to swimming in a twenty-five-yard pool and flipping and pushing off at each end of the pool, you'll likely find that fifty meters is a whole new ball of wax. Take it easy for the first lap or two. Or, during the summer, use the part of the outdoor pool that has a bulkhead and try the twenty-five-meter or twenty-five-yard part first. Meadowbrook is also home to a branch of the Michael Phelps Swim School that offers lessons to adults and youngsters. No, he probably isn't teaching the classes.

Meadowbrook Swim Club, 5700 Cottonworth Ave.
410-433-8300, mbrook.com

GET YOUR DUCKS
IN A ROW

Duckpin bowling is often said to have originated in Baltimore in the 1890s. The balls are smaller than the more popular ten-pin bowling ball, weighing under four pounds. The pins are similarly smaller and you're allowed three balls to try to hit all ten pins. The game is much tougher than ten-pin while being much easier because the smaller balls are easier to handle. The Patterson Bowling Center was opened in 1927 and is the oldest operating facility in the nation. It is home to both league and open play. With the smaller balls, it's a great family outing.

Patterson Bowling Center, 2105 Eastern Ave., Canton (upper Fells Point)
410-675-1011, pattersonbowl.com

TAKE ME OUT
TO THE BALLGAME

Beginning with its revolutionary retro design in 1993, Oriole Park at Camden Yards has set new trends, including the first "scalp-free" zone where you could buy and sell tickets without fear of being scammed or arrested. Of course, those were the days of sold-out games. You can also buy Boog Powell BBQ—with that aroma, just try to resist—and you can tour the stadium, seeing the club level suites, the press level, the scoreboard/JumboTron control room, and the O's dugout. Oh, and be sure to ask about the seventy-five miles of pipeline providing cold beer for your pleasure. Ninety-minute tours are offered daily during the season except when there's a day game. Check the website for the schedule.

Oriole Park at Camden Yards, 333 W Camden St.
410-547-6234, baltimore.orioles.mlb.com

TIP

When you see the numbers 2,131, perhaps as a shrine, it's in reference to the consecutive game record Cal Ripken Jr. set on September 6, 1995, breaking Lou Gehrig's long-standing record of 2,130. He went on to play a total of 2,632 straight games, a record which most likely will not be broken.

PLAY WITH A PURPOSE

Contrary to museums where you hear "shh" and see "please don't touch" signs, this museum is a full-out, total hands-on experience. When the children want to be outside playing and the weather or other conditions say nay, take them to Port Discovery. They can frolic in rooms that include art, water (bring dry clothing to replace the soaked apparel), restaurants, books, and coloring activities. The three-story climbing area with netting, bridges, tubing, and slides is a sure-cure for the excess energy children seem to have in super abundance. Whether your favorite rug rat is an infant, toddler, or preteen—the general age attraction is two through ten—there's an activity geared to his or her interest and capability. Visiting exhibits compliment the permanent ones. To avoid crowds, visit on a Sunday or weekday afternoons. As you can imagine, the place is filled to the gills on school holidays and dollar admission or free days.

Port Discovery Children's Museum, 35 Market Pl., Inner Harbor
410-727-8120, portdiscovery.org

CREWING A TALL SHIP

The *Pride of Baltimore II,* a boat classified as a wooden topsail schooner, was built in 1988 to replace the original *Pride* that sank in a freak microburst in 1986. She sails to distant ports as a goodwill ambassador for Baltimore and Maryland business and tourism. You probably know that you can visit the topsail schooner in the Inner Harbor on a regular basis.

Ah, but do you know that you can sail aboard her, too? Become a crew member, living and working alongside the twelve professional crew members. Catch the waves, stand watch, steer the vessel, and any number of other duties (or not), depending on your interest and ability. The cruises last from four to twenty days and cost from $500 to $1,950. The 2016 cruises went to Norfolk, Virginia; Toronto, Canada; and into the Great Lakes, where she participated in Tall Ships® Duluth 2016 and then went on to other Tall Ship festivals and events. That should be enough to float your boat.

Of course, you can spend less time, either with a deck tour or a day sail when the *Pride II* is in port.

Pride of Baltimore II, 2700 Lighthouse Point East (mailing address)
410-539-1151, pride2.org

RUN FOR THE
BLACK-EYED SUSANS

Thousands gather on the third Saturday of May to watch the Preakness Stakes, the second leg of the Triple Crown, at Pimlico Race Course. It's two weeks after the Kentucky Derby and three weeks before the Belmont Stakes. The week before the race is filled with activities, including behind-the-scenes tours of the stables, a pre-Preakness party where you can meet jockeys, an alibi breakfast that aims to explain why horses haven't run as well as they are or were expected to, a crab derby, a frog hop, and hot air balloons. The track is a one-mile dirt oval, the stables can house about one thousand horses, and the track's human capacity (including the infield) is more than 120,000. Besides horse racing, the course has been home to numerous music concerts, including the Moonrise Festival, an electronic dance festival.

Preakness Stakes, Pimlico Race Course, 5201 Park Heights Ave.
410-542-9400, preakness.com; pimlico.com

TIP

Because black-eyed susans aren't in bloom when the Preakness is run, the flowers used in the blanket placed on the winning horse are actually eighty bunches of Viking daisies that are painted with black lacquer to resemble the state flower. The blanket is eighteen by ninety inches in length.

SHOW ME
THE WAY TO GO HOME

This attraction is part of the Historic Ships collection, although obviously, the lighthouse isn't a ship. However, from 1856 to 1988, the mouth of the Patapsco River was home to two different lighthouses. The forty-foot lighthouse had a fourth-order Fresnel lens—it's been removed—that could be seen for twelve miles. A keeper, and sometimes his family, lived in the house until it was automated in 1949. A short walk for a commute, but rather watery for shopping and land-based errands! The lighthouse was removed from Seven Foot Knoll in 1988 and moved to the Inner Harbor. Once you climb the lighthouse, you'll see information and talk to the docent about the lighthouse and other lighthouses that populated the bay. Although the screwpile design was not exclusive to the bay, it was the primary style used. This one had a central pile and eight others at angles away from the center. This type of pile was necessary so the piles could literally be screwed into the bay's bottom. It's a great place to view the Inner Harbor.

Seven Foot Knoll Lighthouse, Pier 5
410-539-1797, historicships.org/knoll-light

TIPTOE
THROUGH THE TULIPS

Baltimore is famous for many things, and this is right at the top of the list. Created in the 1920s by John W. Sherwood, a local petroleum pioneer and conservationist, the garden contains original tulips that came from the Netherlands. When Sherwood died in 1965, he left the garden and funds to continue maintaining it for a year. After that, the Guilford Association purchased the gardens. Enough about its history. What you want to see are the approximately eighty thousand tulips planted each October that bloom around late April through early May. There are also azaleas, dogwoods, flowering cherries, wisteria, and magnolias. During the summer, come visit the annuals and perennials as they put on their show. At any time, bring a blanket, a picnic basket, your camera, and enjoy the tranquility. You may see a wedding; you're sure to see toddlers and pets. If you have a green thumb and are the least bit jealous of the tulip magnificence, come by on the Saturday morning of Memorial Day weekend, starting at 7 a.m., and you can dig tulip bulbs to your heart's content and pay thirty cents per bulb. Bring your own shovel or spade and a container for the bulbs.

Sherwood Garden, 4100 Greenway
410-889-1717, guilfordnews.com/sherwood

CULTURE AND HISTORY

GRANDMA MOSES
WOULD FIT PERFECTLY

Visionary art is defined as "art produced by self-taught individuals, usually without formal training." Mostly, it's entertaining, educational, and enchanting. Look for mirror art by Bob Benson, an Anne Arundel artist; old-school robots by DeVon Smith; and a rotating statue of Divine. Special programs, both free and for a fee, may celebrate Dr. Martin Luther King Jr. or Valentine's Day, or they may just be a monthly weekend walk-in or reservation-required workshop where you can make a puppet or create a gorgeous mosaic. Participate or watch the annual Kinetic Sculpture Race (see Festivals by Season chapter). Save time to eat at Encantada restaurant.

American Visionary Art Museum, 800 Key Hwy.
410-244-1900, avam.org

Encantada
410-752-1000, encantadabaltimore.com

BALTIMORE BASILICA
OR, THE BASILICA OF THE NATIONAL SHRINE OF THE ASSUMPTION OF THE BLESSED VIRGINIA MARY

In Baltimore's Mount Vernon area, the 210-year-old architecturally striking first cathedral in America, built between 1806 and 1821, was created by John Carroll, the cousin of Charles Carroll, and Benjamin Henry Latrobe, Thomas Jefferson's architect of the Capitol. It's considered an extraordinary example of nineteenth-century architecture, and to me, Latrobe's use of natural light provides a lively, emotionally uplifting interior. A two-year restoration (2004–2006) brought the church to its original design AND made it totally accessible, including a museum. Beside religious services, they offer daily historical tours, concerts, and lectures.

The Baltimore Basilica, 409 Cathedral St.
410-727-3564, americasfirstcathedral.org

WHERE THERE'S SMOKE

Stop by the Box 414 Baltimore City Fire Museum, located in a firehouse built in the mid-1800s, predating the city's paid fire department, for a historic glimpse at firefighting. It has a 117-foot-high Italianate-Gothic bell and clock tower (think Giotto's campanile in Florence, Italy), which is where a volunteer firefighter from the Independent Fire Company would sit to scan the skyline for signs of smoke. The Box 414 name refers to the first alarm box that was pulled for the Great Baltimore Fire of 1904. The collection contains old pumpers, artifacts, memories of the 1904 fire that destroyed fifteen hundred buildings, and the helmets of first responders killed in the line of duty with the deceased member's name and the date and cause of death. On a less serious note, you'll see part of a Playboy Bunny costume from the six-alarm fire in 1969 at the Playboy Club and a scorched bowling pin from the Forest Park Bowling Lanes.

The museum is open on Thursday morning, Friday evening, Sunday afternoon, and by appointment. You'll probably have a retired firefighter for your guide, someone who can tell lots of fascinating stories about the city's firefighting past.

Baltimore City Fire Museum, 414 N Gay St.
410-727-2414, nps.gov/nr/travel/baltimore/b33.htm

MIND-PLEASING TIME

The art collection—thanks to sisters Claribel and Etta Cone who donated works by Matisse (five hundred; they were friends and it's the world's largest private collection), Picasso, Cezanne, van Gogh, Gauguin, Renoir, and other Modernists—totals about one hundred thousand pieces and ranges from Byzantine to current Contemporary with an outdoor sculpture garden. Be sure to notice the flooring in the John Russell Pope building that's almost as breathtaking as the art. The "door" placement in the corners of each room in the Contemporary Wing revolutionized gallery design. Have lunch at Gertrude's, by famed chef John Shields. Free admission.

Baltimore Museum of Art, 10 Art Museum Dr.
443-573-1700, artbma.org

HI HO, HI HO,
IT'S OFF TO WORK WE GO

Baltimore was a MAJOR industrial center, building, manufacturing, and producing everything from motor vehicles to Domino sugar, signaling the city's Industrial Revolution. Most heavy manufacturing has gone, but you can reach into the past at this museum. This is far from a dull history museum. It's fascinating and informative. See how a 1910 pharmacy looked (Noxzema, the skin cream in a cobalt blue jar, has a Baltimore history), walk through the 1865 Platt and Company oyster cannery (the only surviving cannery building in the city), and tour a garment loft. Every corner you turn unveils another marvel (explain a rotary phone to your children or grandchildren) and you're sure to say, "I didn't know that was made here" more than once.

Take a guided tour and talk to the docents, some of whom worked in the original factories. Volunteers are always welcome and your curiosity is bound to be satiated as you learn to research and maintain the collection and help with lectures and field trips.

Baltimore Museum of Industry, 1415 Key Hwy.
410-727-4808, thebmi.org

CLANG, CLANG, CLANG
WENT THE TROLLEY

Today's mass transit is so mass that entire generations don't understand or recognize its predecessors. This museum is dedicated to preserving the city's public transportation history, particularly the street railway days. Public transportation started in Baltimore with horse-drawn cars on rails in 1859. The system modernized with the times, but stopped running in November 1963. You can ride the cars again, on cars from 1900, 1904, 1930 (in service until 1955), and a 1944 Pullman-Standard car, the only regularly operating Pullman PCC in any museum. Built during World War II, paint was used instead of chrome coating. Car 7407 was one of the last streetcars ordered by the city until the new light rail system started. The museum is open every Saturday and Sunday during the summer. Admission includes unlimited rides on the one-and-a-half-mile roundtrip track (Please, can we go again? Please, please. Well, yes.), access to the displays, and a guided carhouse (car barn in some geographic areas) tour.

Baltimore Streetcar Museum, 1901 Falls Rd.
410-547-0264, baltimorestreetcar.org

MAKING HISTORY YOURS

Back in the 1970s and 1980s, the city sold several hundred abandoned, dilapidated houses for anywhere from one dollar to two hundred dollars each—and some said that was overpriced—with the stipulation that the buyer renovate and live in the home. Many years earlier, a once-magnificent home had fallen on hard times and was transformed with Cinderella-like magic (and hard work and money). The Carroll Mansion, a classic example of Federal period architecture, was built around 1811, and Richard Caton and his wife Mary Carroll bought the home for the princely sum of $20,000 in 1818. It was sold in 1855, when it began its decline. It was sold again, in 1868, for one thousand dollars. Fast forward and the mansion was doomed to be demolished, to be replaced by a gas station. Thanks to Mayor Theodore McKeldin, the home was restored and the doors opened and closed again. Finally, it was reopened in 2002 for public viewing. The mansion museum shows antiques that represent the 1820s and 1830s when the Carrolls lived there. Come, take a guided tour, and learn about our forefathers and how they lived and what hard work and determination can do.

Carroll Mansion, 800 E Lombard St.
410-605-2964, carrollmuseums.org

OPEN WIDE

The University Of Maryland School of Dentistry started in 1840, and this little gem of a museum, which has been around since the school opened, holds forty thousand-plus items that explain the history and development of dental science. It's one of the largest and most significant of its kind in the world. While there's lots of serious stuff explaining the connection between good dental hygiene and the health of the rest of your body, perhaps the most enjoyable part for younger ones is the collection of character tooth brushes. You may also see toothpaste commercials, notes about a patron saint of teeth, and that a dentist created cotton candy. Apparently, most people who visit are dentists or hygienists or otherwise related to the dental field. At least, for the rest of us, it's more fun than visiting a dentist. And, how many cities can boast that they have a dental museum? It's here. You should see it.

Dr. Samuel D. Harris National Museum of Dentistry, 31 S Greene St.
410-706-0600, dental.umaryland.edu/museum/index.html

NEARLY 300 YEARS
OF HISTORY IN 10.2 MILES

You can see the city's almost three hundred years of history by starting at the 1900 block of South Charles Street, just north of the Patapsco River and the I-95 ramp flying overhead, and traveling north to the Baltimore Beltway. The 10.2-mile road, dividing Baltimore into east and west, is a history written in architecture (Romanesque, Venetian Palace, Beaux-Arts, Art Deco, Federal, Italianate, Gothic, and more), religion, population density (from magnificent mansions to high-rise apartments), and education. It hikes past Mount Vernon and the first monument to George Washington, Pennsylvania Railroad Station, Highfield House (designed by Ludwig Mies van der Rohe), and green spaces (designed by Frederick Law Olmsted, Senior and Junior), ending ingloriously with a stop sign just a little north of the Beltway. Rather than suggest a particular season (spring tulips at Sherwood Garden; winter with bare trees so you can see the mansions), try each season and be delighted at the surprises.

Historic Charles Street Association, 36 S Charles St., 12th Floor
410-659-7767, charlesstreet.net

TIP

While you can navigate this on your own, you'll do well to pick up John W. McGrain Jr.'s book, *Charles Street: Baltimore's Artery of Elegance*, which helps explain who designed which buildings, what was located in that store front, and takes a stab at what it all means. LOTS of photographs and illustrations.

YOU DON'T EVEN
NEED A LIBRARY CARD TO ENJOY

Enoch Pratt (1808–1896) was a businessman and philanthropist who donated funds to establish the library system, one of the oldest free public library systems in the country. As frequently quoted, Pratt wanted it to be "for all, rich and poor, without distinction of race or color . . . " The original building was replaced in 1933. You should stop by to do library things, and then look around. Besides all the "normal" library functions, you'll notice there are no grand steps—unlike the New York Public Library, for instance—to enter the building. It was ADA compliant from the beginning. Ground-level windows allow light to enter and provide exhibition areas to help entice patrons. There's a koi pond and murals of favorite stories in the children's section, life-size portraits that would make an art museum proud, and an ornate ceiling in the A/V department that speaks of design elements from the Vatican. Rather than trying to figure out what everything is, take a free tour (individuals, small group, or large group) with a general or specific interest. Contact the Chief of the Central Library/State Library Resource Center. Some adjustments might have to be made because of the current multi-million dollar renovation that should be complete in 2018.

Enoch Pratt Free Library, 400 Cathedral St.
410-396-5430, prattlibrary.org

EVEN MORE
SPECTACULAR THAN YOU HEARD

The George Peabody Library of the Peabody Institute of Johns Hopkins University has roughly three hundred thousand books in its collection. It's strengths are in archaeology, British art and architecture, British and American history, biography, English and American literature, Romance languages and literature, Greek and Latin classics, history of science, geography, and exploration and travel, including a large map collection. Impressive. But not nearly as mind-blowing as the library's interior. This spectacular Neo-Renaissance structure was designed by Baltimore architect Edmund G. Lind and opened in 1878. It has five tiers of ornamental cast-iron balconies lifting your eyes from the black and white marble floor to a latticed skylight sixty-one feet above the floor. This atrium over the main reading room has been described as a "Cathedral of Books." When Peabody, a merchant, banker, financier, and philanthropist, created the library, it was "to be maintained for the free use of all persons who desire to consult it." That means you can use the library, although the stacks are closed.

George Peabody Library, 17 E. Mount Vernon Pl.
410-234-494, guides.library.jhu.edu/c.php?g=202582&p=1336208

BROAD STRIPES
AND BRIGHT STARS

You've probably long forgotten your fifth-grade American history class, and you probably have several misconceptions and memory lapses about what happened at the star-shaped Fort McHenry (built in 1798). First, you think the battle, part of the War of 1812, happened in 1812. Wrong, it was September 13–14, 1814. Mary Pickersgill made the huge, thirty-by-forty-two-foot flag that replaced the smaller, seventeen-by-twenty-five-foot storm flag, not Betsy Ross. And, you think Francis Scott Key was a prisoner of war. He was "detained" on a British ship, but he was not a prisoner. He witnessed the battle from that ship and that inspired him to write a poem, *Defence of Fort M'Henry,* that would become the "Star-Spangled Banner," the national anthem of the United States. The fort was in continuous use through World War II.

If you're there at 10:15 a.m., you can help raise the flag, and if you're there at 5 p.m., you can help lower it. Otherwise, watch the movie, hear a ranger talk, and be inspired. The grounds outside the fort are open to all and are a great place for a picnic overlooking the confluence of the Inner Harbor and the Patapsco River.

Fort McHenry, 2400 E Fort Ave.
410-962-4290, nps.gov/fomc/index.htm

SPEND A FEW HOURS
AT YOUR CONVENIENCE

Green Mount Cemetery was Baltimore's first rural or garden cemetery, set on rolling hills, with plenty of nature, lovely gardens, avenues shaded by tall maples, walnuts, sycamores, chestnuts, and beeches, and fine architecture. Among the famous and infamous buried here are the poet Sydney Lanier, philanthropist Johns Hopkins, and actor/assassin John Wilkes Booth, along with two conspirators, Samuel Arnold and Michael O'Laughlen, with pennies bearing Lincoln's image atop their headstones. Congressmen, governors, mayors, business leaders, military personnel from the Civil War forward, and others of note are among the 65,000-plus interred here. The highest elevation is 190 feet above sea level, and you can see the skyline of downtown Baltimore, particularly in the winter. You may walk or drive through the cemetery. Pick up a map for a small fee of the seventy-five-plus most visited graves at the cemetery office on the right of the entrance gate. On May and October Saturday mornings, historian Wayne Schaumburg leads guided tours.

Green Mount Cemetery, 1501 Greenmount Ave.
410-539-0641, greenmountcemetery.com

LEST WE FORGET

Two blocks from the entertaining and educational attractions surrounding the Inner Harbor sits a Holocaust memorial of concrete, steel, and grass dedicated to the 6 million Jews slaughtered during World War II. It was created at the prompting of Baltimore Hebrew school teacher Alvin Fisher because his seventh graders told him they didn't believe the Holocaust happened. The concrete slabs symbolize a train carrying Jews to concentration camps, and the steel gating symbolizes their internment. A statue of a flame consuming emaciated bodies has George Santayana's words: "Those who do not remember the past are destined to repeat it." Signs explain the allegorical references in the memorial's various components.

Baltimore Holocaust Memorial, E Lombard & S Gay Streets
410-542-4850

TRADITION!

This could easily be the Museum of Maryland (and the world) through a Jewish lens, perhaps because the Lloyd Street Synagogue building has had such an interesting history. Constructed in 1845, it was the first synagogue in the state and has since housed two other immigrant congregations, one Jewish and one Lithuanian Roman Catholic. The museum's exhibits are fascinating and approach concepts most people just don't take time to consider. Recent shows have covered such topics as: "Paul Simon: Words & Music," which included handwritten lyrics, Grammy Awards, photos, guitars, and interviews; "Voices of Lombard Street: A Century of Change in East Baltimore," showcasing the neighborhood from the early days of the twentieth century to today; and "ZAP! POW! BAM! The Superhero: The Golden Age of Comic Books," which illustrates how a group of young, largely Jewish, artists created comic books that filled the country with optimism. There's a lighter side to the activities, as demonstrated by the Gefilte Fest, with three chefs showing there's more than one way to gefilte fish.

Jewish Museum of Maryland, 15 Lloyd St.
410-732-6400, jewishmuseummd.org

SHOWING THE WAY
TO SAFETY FOR SEAMEN

The bright red-hulled ship with big white lettering spelling CHESAPEAKE is one of the four Historic Ships of Baltimore in the Inner Harbor: the Lightship 116 *Chesapeake,* the Sloop-of-War *Constellation,* the USS *Torsk* submarine, and the USCGC *Taney.* She's open for one-hour tours (you can tour one or all four ships and the lighthouse) and is part of the overnight program. See the messroom, or dining area, and staterooms, and explore the living conditions, particularly compared to the nearby Seven Foot Knoll Lighthouse. This ship served as a lightship—with a masthead light, foghorn, and bell—at the mouth of the Chesapeake (ergo, the name), weathering two severe hurricanes, until she was replaced by a permanent structure in 1965.

LV 116 *Chesapeake,* Pier 3
410-539-1797, historicships.org

SPLISH SPLASH,
THEY WERE TAKING A BATH

Okay, the National Aquarium is a super aquarium. The design was trendsetting and the collection of swimming (and other) things is outstanding. There are now about twenty thousand animals in more than one hundred exhibits, one of the largest collections on the planet. There's even a petting zoo where you can get up close and personal in the "Living Seashore" exhibit. It's a subtle—or not-too-subtle—reminder that we're the stewards of our planet. My favorite part is the behind-the-scenes tour, where you learn about the "icky, creepy, slimy, and cool," and even more exciting is taking a guided tour before the building opens to the public!

In June 2016, the aquarium announced that it will phase out its dolphin experience. By 2020, the eight Atlantic bottlenose dolphins will be moved to a first-of-its-kind protected, seaside habitat. Between now and then, the dolphins will be taught how to cohabitate with fish and how to catch food for themselves. Webcams will be part of the new habitat, so you'll still be able to see them being dolphins.

National Aquarium in Baltimore, 501 E Pratt St., Inner Harbor
410-576-3800, aqua.org

YOU DON'T NEED
TO BE A NERD

For those who don't understand how science relates to their life, a walk down Main Street in the Maryland Science Center will be enlightening and fun. Solve physics and engineering puzzles as you walk past representations of Baltimore shops, rowhomes, a construction zone, and BWI Airport. Then explore dinosaurs, blue crabs, and life on other planets. See outer space at the planetarium and widen your eyes in the IMAX theater. Half- and full-day summer camp sessions are available for children ages four to thirteen.

Maryland Science Center, 601 Light St., Inner Harbor
410-685-2370 or 410-685-5225 (recording), mdsci.org

FROZEN IN TIME

One nice thing about this museum, unlike any you've probably seen, is it doesn't participate in revisionist history. Yes, we all look through our own experiences, but this museum doesn't candy-coat this aspect of our history. You'll learn about W. E. B. Du Bois, Bea Gaddy, Martin Luther King Jr., Harriet Tubman, Frederick Douglass, Thurgood Marshall, Emmett Till, and about one hundred others. Of particular interest to locals is the Maryland room; however, each year 53 percent of the two hundred thousand people visiting this museum are from out of state. Films, programming, and guided tours are available. Extensive expansion plans are underway.

National Great Blacks in Wax Museum, 1601-03 E North Ave.
410-563-3404, greatblacksinwax.org

GATEWAY TO HISTORY
AND LIVING CULTURE

The longer name for this attraction is the "Reginald F. Lewis Museum of Maryland African American History & Culture," and that covers a lot of ground. Attorney Lewis was the richest African American man in the United States in the 1980s, and his prominence is up there with other Maryland notables including Thurgood Marshall and Frederick Douglass. This museum explores the lives of Maryland politicians, artists, religious leaders, military personnel, musicians, athletes, and people of other walks of life through art, textiles, photographs, books, about two thousand jazz records from the 1920s through the 1950s, and other items. Three major galleries hold permanent and temporary exhibits about family and community, labor, and art and intellect. There's also a large collection of African art and material culture.

Reginald F. Lewis Museum, 830 E Pratt St.
443-263-1800, lewismuseum.org

YOU'LL BE AMAZED
ONCE YOU'RE INSIDE

The red brick Phoenix Shot Tower, also known as the Old Baltimore Shot Tower, was built in 1828 with an estimated 1.1 million bricks in less than six months. The Phoenix Shot Tower Company of Baltimore built the 215-foot structure, which made it the tallest building in the country until Manhattan's Trinity Church spire was rebuilt in 1846. Lead and additives were hauled up the tower in a dumbwaiter, heated on a wood fire, and then poured through a sieve to land in a quenching tank of cool water at the bottom. They became spherical during the descent, making pellets similar to BBs. The tower, one of four owned by the company, made as much as 2.5 million pounds of shot a year. The shot was used for hunting game and waterfowl, a huge Chesapeake industry. It closed in 1892. Tower tours are offered at 4 p.m. on the weekends, and 10 a.m. to noon on summer weekends. Panels explain the tower's history and the 1924 preservation work. The most amazing aspect is how tall it is once you're inside.

Phoenix Shot Tower, 801 E Fayette St.
410-605-2964, carrollmuseums.org/explore/phoenix-shot-tower

TIP

You can climb one flight of steps to the mezzanine for a slightly better perspective. Negotiations are in the works to retrofit the 305 spiral steps to the top so you can make the climb. You can buy a shot tower game on iTunes, suitable for fifth graders, to benefit the full restoration fundraising campaign.

OH, SAY CAN YOU SEE

You've seen the American flag at the Smithsonian Institution's National Museum of American History in Washington, D.C. You've been to Fort McHenry to hear the story of the storm flag and the garrison flag that Francis Scott Key saw after the British attack on the fort. Now, it's time to see where the flag was made. Mary Pickersgill, whom you now know made the flag, not Betsy Ross, with the help of her mother, Rebecca Young, and her daughter, Caroline, created a flag business. You can tour the building, see some original possessions, and learn more about the flag and its creation. Young ones can design a flag and fly it on the gallery's flagpole, cook at a replica kitchen, and participate in other activities. You can measure yourself against the two-foot tall stars and try to lift a weight and pulley that's comparable to the flag's weight, about eighty to eighty-five pounds. For serious question-askers, schedule your visit for Wednesday, Thursday, or Saturday, when a docent is available with answers.

Star-Spangled Banner Flag House, 844 E Pratt St.
410-837-1793, flaghouse.org

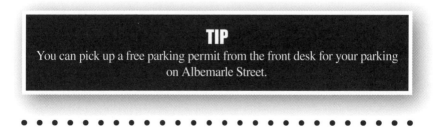

TIP
You can pick up a free parking permit from the front desk for your parking on Albemarle Street.

ON A
CLEAR DAY

The World Trade Center, designed by I. M. Pei, is the tallest pentagonal building east of the Mississippi and the exception to the ten-story building height limit established for buildings directly around the Inner Harbor. The 360-degree view from the twenty-seventh-floor observation level lets you see the city's attractions, the harbor, and forever on a clear day. Binoculars and photo-map guides help you identify what you're seeing, and exhibits help you understand Baltimore history.

World Observation Level, 401 E Pratt St., Inner Harbor
410-837-VIEW, viewbaltimore.org

A DAY THAT WILL
LIVE IN INFAMY

One of the four Historic Ships of Baltimore, the USCGC *Taney,* along with the Sloop-of-War *Constellation,* the USS *Torsk* submarine, and the Lightship *Chesapeake,* is located in the Inner Harbor and is open for one-hour tours (you can tour one or all four ships and the lighthouse). You see the deck, the bridge, and below decks where the men slept and ate and where the officers had their quarters. The *Taney* was a United States Coast Guard Cutter that is the last ship floating that fought in the attack on Pearl Harbor (she was in Honolulu Harbor, not Pearl). She saw action in the Atlantic and Pacific theaters of war and in the conflict with Vietnam. Another interesting assignment was as part of the search team looking for aviatrix Amelia Earhart. Her last assignments found her patrolling the Atlantic Ocean waters for drug smugglers.

USCGC *Taney,* Pier 5
410-539-1797, historicships.org

BOOM!

The US Sloop-of-War *Constellation* is one of the four Historic Ships of Baltimore, along with the US Submarine *Torsk,* the US Coast Guard Cutter *Taney,* and the Lightship *Chesapeake,* all located in the Inner Harbor. The *Constellation* (in service from 1797 to 1853) shows life at sea, particularly during the illegal slave trade leading up to the Civil War. Go on your own or take a one-hour guided tour and engage in hands-on activities that almost make you believe you were there as she captured the slave ship *Cora,* rescuing 705 Africans. Or, you may hear a lesson about the guns onboard and maybe have your eardrums assaulted as one is fired.

USS *Constellation,* Pier 1 301 E Pratt St.
410-539-1797, historicships.org

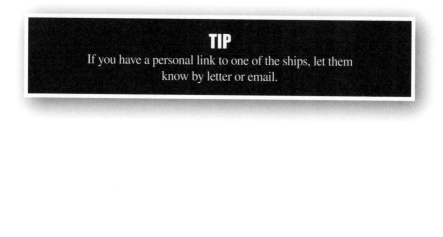

TIP
If you have a personal link to one of the ships, let them know by letter or email.

DISCOVERY TIME

Lots of places say they have something for everyone and, fortunately, the Walters Art Museum fits the bill—even for those who don't "like" art. From mummies to suits of armor, and from the third millennium BC to the early twentieth century, they have it. If you like Old Masters, Art Nouveau jewelry, Egyptian, Greek, Roman, and more, plan to spend a lot of time. They make ancient modern, as witnessed by an exhibit they had about recycling and reusing parts in their medieval art treasures. It's all thanks to William and Henry Walters, who collected and then donated. Docents go through a year-long training program, so they should be able to answer any question you can ask. Best "hidden" thing is the restoration area. No admission fee to the museum.

The Walters Art Museum 600 N Charles St.
410-547-9000
thewalters.org

DIVE! DIVE! DIVE!

One of the four Historic Ships of Baltimore, the USS *Torsk,* along with the Sloop-of-War *Constellation,* the US Coast Guard Cutter *Taney,* and the Lightship *Chesapeake,* located in the Inner Harbor, is the one with the teeth on its bow. You can tour one or all four. This baby could do 20.25 knots on the surface and 8.75 knots when submerged and held a crew of ten officers and seventy-one enlisted personnel. Yep, tight quarters. She's a Tench class sub with improved interior machinery and blast tank arrangements, one of two still located in the United States.

If you've dreamed of being a submariner, you and nineteen to thirty-one friends can spend the night on the *Torsk* (you can also spend the night on the *Constellation* and the *Taney*). You learn about periscopes, torpedoes, buoyance, and how subs exist below the surface.

USS *Torsk,* Pier 3
410-539-1797, historicships.org

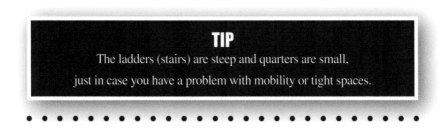

TIP
The ladders (stairs) are steep and quarters are small,
just in case you have a problem with mobility or tight spaces.

ONLY A BIRD
IN A GILDED CAGE

She sits there like a well-loved dowager, mannerly, with a slight twinkle in the windows that are her eyes. Behind that calm exterior is a treasure of stories and riches from the Gilded Age. The former home of Alice and John Garrett, donated to Johns Hopkins University, the gild is literally there in the bathroom fixtures. The art is by Picasso, Degas, Modigliani, and others, along with contemporary art on exhibit. There is a theater, a library of rare books and manuscripts, and forty-eight luxurious rooms filled with fine and decorative arts. Italian-style gardens surround the home that sits on twenty-six acres. Regular programming includes concerts, films, and lectures. There's a surprise with each footstep and in all the nooks and crannies. Most enjoyable is the lack of crowds so docents can answer your every question.

Evergreen Museum and Library, 4545 N Charles St.
410-516-0341, museums.jhu.edu

THIS WAS HERE FIRST

Yes, this was the first monument dedicated to America's first president, George Washington. Both this one, with its cornerstone placed in 1815, and the one southwest of here, dedicated in 1885, were designed by architect Robert Mills. This one recently had a $6.5 million restoration, thanks to the Mount Vernon Place Conservancy. A two-hundred-year-old cornerstone time capsule was uncovered (they knew it was somewhere) with newspapers, coins, a copy of his presidential farewell address, and a copy of the Declaration of Independence. You may climb the 227 steps, measuring 130 feet, Wednesday through Sunday, with timed tickets, with twenty minutes allowed for you to climb, look around, take photos, catch your breath, and descend. However, only five people are allowed to climb at one time.

The monument is home base for dozens of events (arts, books, flowers, etc.) every year, with the highlight coming the first Thursday in December as it becomes a marble Christmas tree lit with LED lights, designating the start of the Christmas season. There are fireworks and vendors with a variety of foodstuffs available. Oh, and the lights are a different color pattern each year.

Washington Monument, Mount Vernon Place
410-396-1049, baltimore.org/article/washington-monument

TIP

If you're not up to the climb,
you can have a virtual experience at
mvpconservancy.org/digital-exhibits

SHOPPING AND FASHION

BIBLIOPHILES WANTED

Even with all the ways people can read books today, people still like to hold a book and turn pages and maybe make notes and return to their old friends time and time again. Baltimore has a fairly good supply of brick-and-mortar stores, thank goodness. One store that's particularly dear is the Book Thing. When you're ready to downsize, the Book Thing will take the books that you can't sell and that Goodwill and the library don't want. Tax deductible. They provide books to anyone for free. As many as you want. Free. If you go in looking for a specific book, you may be disappointed. Look around and maybe you'll find something that will change your life. They only ask that you not resell it. Unfortunately, a disastrous fire in January 2016 destroyed the place. Showing what good neighbors we have, volunteers have given time to clean and paint and process the new supply of books that neighbors have donated to refill the shelves. The Book Thing is due to reopen in late fall 2016.

Book Thing of Baltimore, 3001 Vineyard Ln.
410-662-5631, bookthing.org

GENTRIFICATION
HAS ARRIVED

Only two miles from downtown Baltimore, you'd almost think you're somewhere totally different. Legend says Irish merchant John O'Donnell started trading with a port in China called Canton in the late 1700s, thus the name. Instead of blue-collar homes and industrial complexes, there's a dog park, apartment buildings, new townhouses, restaurants, and bars that please a twenty-something population. The Shops at Canton Crossing is the nearest mall to the downtown area with the requisite chain stores. They range from Five Below to Harris Teeter and service businesses including a cleaners and a mail package store. For a touch of the individual and unique, try 2910 On The Square, where you can find two floors of home decor, Baltimore memorabilia, apparel, local art, jewelry, Judaica, all things crabby, and so much more. Stop by Canton Games, where you go for board games, comic books and graphic novels, collectibles, and a place where like-minded people come to play games. Befitting the area's demographics, Cloud 9 Clothing at the Can Company sells eclectic women's clothing, accessories, and jewelry. They also have stores in Hampden and the Shops at Kenilworth.

Canton Community Association
410-342-0900, cantoncommunity.org

OVERLOOKING
EVERYTHING

When you see a photograph of the Inner Harbor, it was almost certainly taken from the top of Federal Hill Park. Walk a few blocks south and you'll find a large variety of eclectic, locally owned boutiques with clothing, accessories, and other necessities of life (or things you didn't know you wanted or needed.) A variety of art galleries are ready to lure you in so you can find that perfect piece that will finish your new decorating scheme. You could also wind up with a tattoo (Brightside, brightsidebaltimore.com), new and antiquarian books (Book Escape, thebookescape.com), linens and gifts (Phina's, phinas.com), home décor (Pandora's Box, facebook.com/shoppandorasboxboutique), furniture (Shofer's, shofers.com), and some delicious edibles from the Cross Street Market (operating since 1846).

Federal Hill, 42 E Cross St.
410-727-4500, fedhill.org

BIPPITY BOPPITY BOO

If you think Baltimore is only the mean and dangerous city that seems to make the news, then you haven't been to Harbor East in the past few years. This twelve-block area is home to tony boutiques, high-end restaurants (a few are included in the Food and Drink section), and hotel and residential accommodations that will please the most discerning. The decrepit warehouses from a century ago have been transformed, Cinderella-style, into buildings that hold a combination of high-end brand names and the socially conscious businesses. So, you have Allen Edmonds men's shoes and Warby Parker eyewear. You'll find Brooks Brothers, Free People, Bin 604 wines, BMore Betty (which puts a Beverly Hills spin to a resale boutique), Anthropologie, and Whole Foods Market. There's even a massive statue—largest in the city—dedicated to the Katyn Forest Massacre, a little-known event where two hundred thousand Poles were killed in 1940.

Harbor East, 650 S Exeter St.
410-779-4700, harboreast.com

EVERYTHING OLD
IS NEW AGAIN

Whether you refer to it as Fell's Point or Fells Point, the area is in a constant state of revival and reinvention. It's a small area, centered around the old Broadway Market and Broadway Square, with cobblestone streets and an amazing history. While most of the storefronts on Broadway are restaurants and bars, wander around a bit and you'll find fashions, toys, antiques, home décor, jewelry, hats, and other odds and ends. There's even a psychic. What you probably won't see are chain stores that you can find anywhere else. Fells Point Creamery is a tiny but spectacular place for a scoop of deliciousness. Fans of the *Homicide: Life on the Streets* television show will recognize a lot of buildings. The 1914 cargo hold and then recreation center and dance hall that was used as the police headquarters (and actually did house the former headquarters of Pat Moran Casting, with Pat doing all the local casting for the show, as well as for Barry Levinson and John Waters movies) has been empty since 1999. It is undergoing massive renovation. The Under Armour Company is taking the Recreation Pier and turning it into a $60 million, 128-room hotel with a pool and restaurant.

Fells Point Main Street, P.O. Box 38245
410-675-8900, fellspointmainstreet.org

A LOCAVORE'S DREAM

With its big-city designation (twenty-first largest by population),
it's nice to know you can find locally grown fruits, vegetables, and
flowers; locally made cheeses; baked goods; and seafood, including
great crabs, at local farmers markets. You can often find handmade
items, and, if nothing else, they're great for people watching. Each
one is different, geared toward the area, so if you want something
specific and it's not in your neighborhood market, try another one.
You may be pleasantly surprised. Remember to bring cash. Many
vendors do not accept credit or debit cards. This is in addition to
another half-dozen public markets that are open all year and sell
goods other than foodstuffs.

Farmers Markets

Baltimore Museum of Industry Farmers Market, 1415 Key
Hwy.,Saturday, May through October, 9 a.m.–1 p.m.
thebmi.org/page/bmi_farmers%27_market

Druid Hill Farmers Market, 3100 Swan Dr.
Wednesday, June through September, 3:30–7:30 p.m.
druidhillpark.org/market.html

Fells Point Farmers Market
Broadway and Thames Streets
Saturday, May through November, 7:30 a.m.–12:30 p.m.

Pratt Street Farmers Market
Corner of Pratt and Light Streets
Thursday, May through October, 11 a.m.–2 p.m.

Waverly Farmers Market, East 32nd and Barclay Streets
Saturday, all year, 7 a.m.–12 noon
32ndstreetmarket.org

Public Markets

Avenue Market, 1700 Pennsylvania Ave.
Monday through Saturday 7 a.m.–6 p.m.

Broadway Market, 1640-41 Aliceanna St.
Monday through Saturday 7 a.m.–6 p.m.

Cross Street Market, 1065 S Charles St.
Monday through Saturday 7 a.m.–7 p.m.

Hollins Street Market, 26 S Arlington Ave.
Tuesday through Saturday 7 a.m.–6 p.m.

Lexington Market, 400 W Lexington St.
Monday through Saturday 8:30 a.m.–6 p.m.

Northeast Market, 2101 E Monument St.
Monday through Saturday 7 a.m.–6 p.m.

IT'S THE "AVENUE," HON

The four blocks of 36th Street between Chestnut Avenue and Falls Road are known as "The Avenue," and it's where almost everything that happens in Hampden happens. Just look for the large pink flamingo over Café Hon and you know you're in Hampden, hon. Quirky boutiques, eateries, a shop that sells shoes and chocolate, another one that features comic books, and other shops that sell everything from antiques to sporting goods to adult toys to vintage clothing. One place your sweet tooth will love, although they have both savory and sweet offerings, is Dangerously Delicious Pies (dangerouspiesbalt.com). Hang around a bit and enjoy First Fridays, HampdenFest, Halloween in Hampden, HonFest, Miracle on 34th Street, the Mayor's Christmas Parade, and other community activities. No promises, but be on the lookout for film director John Waters. He's been known to frequent the area.

Hampden Shopping District, 36th Street
hampdenmerchants.com

CULTURE AND COUTURE

The Mount Vernon area is well known for its cultural attractions, architecture, and gardens. It's also a treasure trove for someone looking for something unusual and wonderful from a locally owned or family-operated (or both) shop. You can start at the Walters Art Museum gift shop (thewalters.org), then stop by the tiny bookshop at the American Institute of Architects (aiabalt.org), and then wander into Dubey's Art and Antiques (dubeysantique. wordpress.com). Shops that sell flowers, menswear, clocks and clock repair, books, and other essentials are scattered throughout the area. A People United (apeopleunited.com) deals in incense, accessories, clothing, and more. Perrin and Associates Fine Violins (perrinviolins.com) and Ted's Musicians Shop (tedsmusiciansshop. wix.com/tedsmusiciansshop#!) provide your musical needs. Milk and Honey Market (milkandhoneybaltimore.com/), Eddie's of Mount Vernon (eddiesofmtvernon.com/), and OK Natural Food Store (oknaturalfoods.com/) provide daily food essentials.

Mount Vernon Belvedere Association, 1 E Chase St.
410-528-1919, mvba.org

FESTIVALS BY SEASON

WINTER

SPRING

ACTIVITIES
BY SEASON

WINTER

SPRING

INDEX